Chapters from
Medieval History

Chapters from Medieval History

compiled by
Dorothy Harrer

The phrase "Middle Ages" describes Europe between the fall of Rome in 476 CE and the beginning of the Renaissance in the 14th century, a time when European thinkers, writers, and artists began to look back and celebrate the art and cultures of ancient Greece and Rome. They dismissed the period after the fall of Rome as a "Middle" or even "Dark" age in which no scientific accomplishments were made, no great art produced, no great leaders born. They argued that the people of the Middle Ages misspent the advancements of their predecessors and mired themselves instead in "barbarism and religion" [Edward Gibbon, 18th-century English historian].

This way of thinking about the era in the "middle" of the fall of Rome and the rise of the Renaissance prevailed until relatively recently. However, today's scholars note that the era was as complex and vibrant as any other.

Printed with support from the Waldorf Curriculum Fund

Published by:
Waldorf Publications at the
Research Institute for Waldorf Education
351 Fairview Avenue Suite 625
Hudson, NY 12534

Title: *Chapters from Medieval History*
Author: Dorothy Harrer
Copy editor/proofreader: Gene Talbot
Layout: Ann Erwin
Cover image: Community Images, Internet Archive

© 2024 Waldorf Publications
ISBN # 978-1-963686-04-3

Contents

Setting the Stage

Sons of Ishmael	8
The Arabian and Iberian Peninsulas	9
A Little Bit about Spain	11
Migrations	13
The Germanic People	13
The Franks	15

The Rise of Islam

Mohammed Ben Abdallah Ben Abdul-Muttalib	17
Passages from the Koran	24
The Arabs Advance	26
Arabism	29
The Religion of the Crescent	34

The Early Middle Ages

More about the Franks	37
Pepin the Short	38
Charlemagne	39
The Song of Roland	46
The Age of Disorder	55
The Medieval Castle and the Monastery	55
Priestly Power and Kingly Power	61
Manuscripts and Cathedrals	63
Henry IV and Gregory VII	66
The Culture of the Moors	68

Excerpts from the History of England

Uthyr	71
Arthur	73
Alfred the Great	75
Edward the Confessor	77
The Normans	77
William of Normandy	78
The Plantagenets	79

The Crusades

The Start of the Crusades	83
"Deus Vult"	86
The Crusades	88
The Hospitalers and the Templars	93
The Results of the Crusades	94

Streams of Human Development

Frederick I (Barbarossa)	97
Henry VI	98
Frederick II	99
Powers of the Roman Church	105
The Towns	107
Waldensians and Albigensians	110
Francis of Assisi	112
The Hundred Years' War and Jeanne d'Arc	114

Attributes 117

Setting the Stage

The Sons of Ishmael

Abraham had a son, Ishmael, born of an Egyptian maid named Hagar. Ishmael means "God heareth." Sarah also bore a son to Abraham. He was Isaac. Sarah prevailed upon Abraham to banish Hagar and Ishmael, lest Ishmael become Abraham's heir instead of Isaac.

"And Abraham rose up early in the morning and took bread and a bottle of water and gave it unto Hagar and gave her the child and sent her away: and she departed and wandered in the wilderness of Beersheba.

"And the water in the bottle was spent, and she cast the child under one of the shrubs. And she sat over against him and lifted up her voice and wept.

"And God heard the voice of the lad and the angel of God called to Hagar out of heaven and said to her,

"'What aileth thee, Hagar? Fear not, for God hath heard the voice of the lad where he is. Arise, lift up the lad, and hold him in thy hand: for I will make him a great nation.'

"And God opened her eyes, and she saw a well of water, and filled the bottle with water, and gave the lad drink.

"And God was with the lad and he grew, and he dwelt in the wilderness and became, as he grew up, an archer. And he dwelt in the wilderness of Paran: and his mother took him a wife out of the land of Egypt."

– Genesis, Chapter 21

The site where Hagar found the well became the city of Mecca, a holy place for the Sons of Ishmael, the Arabs. In Mecca was built the Kaaba, and the guardians of the Kaaba were a tribe called the Koreish (or Quraish). The Kaaba, a cubic building containing a Black Stone, contained also idols of the gods of the Arabs which were Sun, Moon, rain, trees, spirits of nature and animals.

The Arabian and Iberian Peninsulas

The Arabian Peninsula, at the southwest end of Asia, is a desert region flanked by extensive land areas beyond the narrow waters of the Red Sea and the Persian Gulf. It lies in the path of prevailing easterly winds that carry dry air from across the continent of Asia.

The scanty rainfall in Arabia occurs over the mountains of Yemen that are high enough to deflect the winds to cooler regions of the sky where the moisture they have gathered over the Arabian Sea condenses and falls as rain.

The Iberian Peninsula, at the southwest end of Europe, is surrounded by water and lies in the path of prevailing westerly winds that bear moisture from over the Atlantic Ocean. When the summer sun is high, rain falls in the Cantabrian Mountains and along the coast of Portugal; but the hot sun dries out the winds that blow from the west, so that Spain suffers a rainless summer. In the winter, cooler air allows the winds to carry their moisture further inland and rain falls in Spain where the parched earth now blossoms with plant life.

Both peninsulas are mainly plateau regions where the main occupation became the shepherding of flocks.

There are no rivers in the Arabian Peninsula, but Spain is watered by the rivers that flow from the snows and rains of the mountain regions to the surrounding seas. Spain's mineral resources, iron, mercury, copper, and silver,

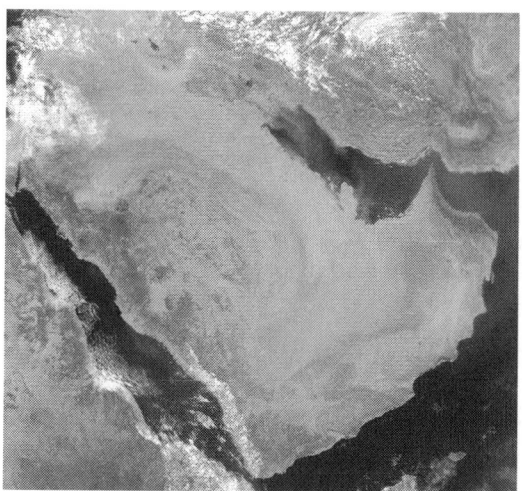
Arabian Peninsula

Iberian Peninsula

allowed her the wealth to become a great sea power. Spain guards the gates to the western ocean. Arabia lies along the ancient trade routes between Asia and Europe. Only in recent times has oil, her great mineral resource, taken the place of sand.

Such are the two regions where the important drama of the spreading of Arabian culture was enacted, with its threats and gifts to Western civilization.

A Little Bit about Spain

The Iberian Peninsula was named after the people, the Iberians, who were the original inhabitants first conquered by Hamilcar Barca of Carthage. Barcelona was named for him. But many Iberians had fled from the Carthaginians into the Cantabrian Mountains. They are the Basques who dwell on both the French and Spanish sides of these mountains, but they speak their own language, unlike any other in the world. The Carthaginians taught the natives to mine metals that were taken to Carthage and forged into weapons.

Then came the Romans. The way of entry into Spain for their armies was the lowland at the end of the Pyrenees, and they sent their war prisoners to work in the Spanish mines. The Romans built fine roads throughout the peninsula, and aqueducts and sewers. Towns became Romanized. Romans married the native Iberians and brought up their children to be Romans. There were good laws and good government under Rome for 500 years, with the development of schools, businesses, comfort, wealth—in other words civilized living.

Then, pushing down through the same "door" at the east end of the Pyrenees through which the Romans had come, came a new, rough people from the North: tall, fair, bearded, young in development, like children bursting out of school and ready for anything exciting.

First came the Vandals, pillaging, looting, destroying much, settling for a while in Vandalusia (Andalusia) in the south, later moving on to Carthage, and even later back to attack Rome.

Then came the Goths and Alani to settle in Goth-Alania (Catalonia) and then move further in as the Vandals left. They did not burn or pillage but paid no attention to Roman laws or Roman roads. They took what land they wished along the coast but avoided the Roman towns and large estates. Living side by side with the Roman people, the Goths gradually intermarried with the Romans and adopted their ways. Their descendants became the early Spaniards to whom the missionaries came and converted them to Christianity. Latin, the language of the Church, became their language. Toledo was the Gothic capital.

The Royal Family, descended from Odin, were the Bältir from whom the King must be chosen. This family ruled in Spain for 200 years. They lived luxuriously, and became lazy and corrupt. In 708 CE Wittich the King was deposed for his tyranny and his cousin Roderick was crowned in his stead.

Near Toledo stood an ancient tower above a cave. Above the iron gate, with many locks, was engraved, "The King who opens this cave and discovers its wonders will learn both good and evil." Many kings had gone as far as the opening but were terrified out of their senses by a tremendous noise within the cavern. Roderick decided to try his fortune at the tower.

The gate was opened. By torchlight the King went into the cave and came to a magnificent hall where stood a bronze statue of fierce aspect holding a battleax and striking the ground with a tremendous noise. The King was bold and spoke to the statue, bidding it cease, to give him time to examine the cave, promising to do it no harm. The figure became still and the King examined the place and found these words written on the wall, "Unhappy King, thou hast entered in an evil hour. By strange nations thou shalt be dispossessed and thy people degraded." Then he saw, written on the shoulders and breast of the statue, "I do my office. I call upon the Arabs."

The King left the cave in haste and closed up the entrance with earth, but at midnight a fearful sound was heard. The whole ancient tower was discovered to have cracked down to its foundations.

Migrations

The Germanic People

In the first century BC, while Augustus Caesar was Emperor, a people were journeying westward from out of Asia, stopping here and there to graze their herds. Their ancestors had come from the West, led by Manu, and their legends speak of their ancestor, Ingvas, one of the three sons of Manu whom they believed to be the first man. One of the stopping places where they paused in their journeying was along the shores of the Black Sea, east of the River Don.

The name of their leader was Odin, and they called their home on the banks of the Don, Asgard. It is said that this human Odin dreamed that far to the west he should find a better home for his people, a "Manheim." As the all-conquering Roman power was reaching out to disturb them in Asgard, Odin led his tribe to the northwest to find the dreamed-of Manheim. This journey led to new settlements on the Great Plain of Europe, in Saxe-land south of the North Sea, and in Angle-land to the east across the Elbe River, where Odin established his son, Baldur, as ruler. The fist of land that thrusts itself up between the North Sea and the Baltic Sea, now called Jutland, was Jute-land. Here a third settlement was under Odin's rule. Odense (Odens-öe, or Odin's Island), in present-day Denmark, was his capital. These three divisions of the followers of this ancient Odin became in time the Saxons, the Angles, and the Jutes who, together with the Goths, the Vandals, the Lombards, and the Franks, were part of the Teutonic race.

The new Manheim was not exactly a garden-land, but a land of vast forests and dismal swamps, washing in from the ocean, in which there were many dangerous quicksands. What is now the low country, the Netherlands, was once the marshes of Saxe-land. What is now the rich farming country of northern Germany was the wet, swampy forest of Angle-land. And the land of the Jutes is now the pastures of Denmark.

In these regions and in those times the winter was harsher, colder, and wetter, with more fog and rain and snow than there is today. This was because of the swamps, rivers and forests. For the people who settled there, their idea of the underworld was that of a "hell of water," not of fire as for the Arabs. The forests were so thick that the squirrels could leap from tree to tree for miles. Such were the land and climate wherein people who had been nomads on the hot plains of Asia settled down and lived.

Their houses were of wood or wattles (woven twigs and branches) with steep, thatched roofs of reeds. These houses were grouped together for protection in what were called burgs, tuns (towns), or hams (hamlets). Such place names as we know derive from such terms: Edinburgh, Edenton, Durham.

Led by their chieftains or kings, each tribe consisted of about 100 families. The men were hunters and warriors who pledged themselves to follow their chief, the bravest of them all, in return for the plunder and booty he promised them. At times 50 tribes banded together in armies of 5000 to win, in great force, the victories over Rome.

For 1200 years Rome had been the force that built a world civilization in which people lived according to law in peace and comfort, protected by the Roman legions that guarded the boundaries of the Roman Empire. In Gaul and Britain there were fine country houses and homesteads, trade, farming, art, and literature. The Roman world was like an old man who wanted nothing more than to live in peace and enjoy the good gifts of life; but outside the carefully guarded frontiers of the Empire "vast masses of hungry, savage men surged and schemed" and bore southward into Roman lands. "A long night was to fall upon the world."

The comfort-loving Romans did not have the force to withstand the invaders, the Germani, great of body with fierce blue eyes, long reddish hair twisted in a knot on top of their heads, long beards, tight-fitting trousers, and cloaks fastened at the throat with clasps. They had tremendous strength for fighting but little interest in hard work, which was done by the women. The women built the houses and grew patches of grain, doing the field work, the household work, and, when the tribe moved on, followed the warriors in wagons, herding the animals along.

No warrior dared surpass his chief in bravery. The only weapons were the spear and the shield. To lose them was the greatest dishonor. The tribal councils were always to plan raids. When the warriors approved a chief's proposals, they clashed their weapons. They could neither read nor write, they did not understand trade, and their system of justice was cruel. Men were judged guilty or innocent by combat, ordeal, and/or compurgation. The winner in combat was considered to be the innocent one. In the ordeal, the one accused of a crime was made to walk through fire, or to put his hand into molten metal, or he was thrown into water. If he were burned, or if he floated in the water, showing that the water rejected him, he was judged guilty. Judgment by compurgation required a number of persons to make an oath claiming the innocence of an accused person; then he was deemed innocent. However, if it was later proved that he was guilty, those who swore to his innocence would have to suffer the punishment as well.

The Franks

One of the Germanic tribes called themselves "the free," or the Franks. In most ways they were like the other tribes, but whereas these others passed on and through the lands they invaded and lost themselves among the Romans, the Franks kept the territories they won and maintained their rear guards and their lines of communication, so that as they spread out into new lands they could not be isolated and surrounded by any enemies. So they gained permanent footholds and settled down as masters of the land.

In Gaul they found Roman palaces, gardens, luxuries, and good farming country. Taking over the estates, and with servants who were their captives, the Frankish chieftains did nothing themselves but, as of old, contrived that someone else would do the work for them. They turned over the management of their estates to their "counts." The Frankish "kings" dressed in Roman robes and were called "long-haired dolls." They lived in such seclusion that they were seen by their subjects only when they rode in their regal ox carts from one of their estates to another. A king's authority was really in the hands of an assistant who was called the "Mayor of the Palace" and whose son succeeded him in office. As they became property owners, the Franks began to use, for the first time, money as the Romans did, and the only way they could hold onto their property was to adopt Roman laws.

The Rise of Islam

Mohammed Ben Abdallah Ben Abdul-Muttalib
(570–633 CE)

Abdul-Muttalib was a Koreish Chief in Mecca. The father of eighteen children, he had made a vow to sacrifice one of his sons to the idols of the Kaaba, and this was Abdallah, 24 years old, and the one that he loved the most. The other Koreish chieftains rose against this action and consulted an *arrafa* (witch) who declared that instead of Abdallah one hundred camels should die. Abdallah, thus saved, married Amina nine days later.

Their son was born five days after the death of the Roman Emperor Justinian. This boy was Mohammed. His father had died before his birth. His mother died when Mohammed was six years old. (In Arabic, the term "Ben" in a name means "son of." Thus, Mohammed Ben Abdallah Ben Abdul-Muttalib indicates Mohammed's parentage, the names of his father and his father's father.)

Mohammed was put out to nurse until his third year with Halima, the wife of a herdsman. Many wonders were said to have happened. Halima's flocks and herds increased tenfold, and her fields bore a great harvest. The child had strange fits and convulsions and in the third year was returned to his mother. His grandfather took care of him when his mother died, for two years. When the grandfather died, his uncle, Abu Talib, took the boy in and gave him a father's care.

At 12 years of age, Mohammed accompanied Abu Talib on a caravan journey to Syria where a Christian monk is said to have foretold his future greatness. As he grew up, Mohammed took care of his uncle's flocks and often journeyed with the caravans across the desert, learning to know its dangers and making contacts with the Jews and Christians. He could not read or write, but the people he met taught him much. At 25 years of age he took charge of some caravans for Khadija, the wealthy widow of a merchant. He carried out his assignment so well and showed such honesty that Khadija (40 years old) married him. Now he was wealthy instead of poor.

For more than ten years Mohammed lived as a merchant but with little success or content. Often, deep in thought, he withdrew to a mountain cave not far from Mecca, sometimes alone and sometimes with Khadija. It was a gloomy

Mohammed Ben Abdallah

neighborhood of naked rocks and yawning precipices. There were no trees, no shade, no grass, no sound of falling water. From Jews and Christians he had heard of the worship of one God. He suffered to think of the idols worshiped by his people.

When he was about 40 years old, he had a vision in the gloomy cave. The Angel Gabriel approached him and commanded him to give a message to his people. A light seemed to enter into him. At first he was afraid that a demon was playing a trick on him. His face streaming with perspiration, he went to his wife and told her what had happened. She believed that it was no demon and so comforted him. Soon the Angel appeared a second time and told Mohammed that he had been chosen by God to spread abroad the revelation of Heaven. Mohammed now believed and announced that Allah, the Lord of Heaven and Earth, had chosen him to be His messenger to inform men of His Holy Will.

For three years he preached and taught the Word of God (given to him by Gabriel) only to his relatives and close friends. In the fourth year his vision commanded him to appear publicly as a prophet and he addressed himself to the men of his tribe, the Koreish, in the name of one God and threatened them with the fire of Hell if they did not renounce their idols and turn to the one God. The Koreish, fearing to lose their priestly honor and position, became his first enemies, and from them he was often in danger of his life. He was outlawed and, with his followers and his uncle, took refuge for three years in a strong castle outside the city. The more he was persecuted, the more followers he won. He returned to Mecca to continue to preach "Islam" (submission to God).

After the deaths of his uncle and his wife, he again had a vision. In spirit he was borne on a winged horse to the Temple in Jerusalem and from there was escorted by Gabriel through seven heavens into the presence of God Who proclaimed him as the crown and aim of creation. Then the Lord revealed to Mohammed everything that "believers" should do to serve Him. After this

Mohammed descended to Jerusalem on the winged horse and returned to Mecca, "thus accomplishing in one night a journey of many thousand years."

What was this religion, this "surrender," to be? It demanded acceptance of the one God and Mohammed as His messenger and the performance of prayers five times a day, that believers give one-fortieth of their property to the poor, that they fast through the month of Ramadan (the ninth month of the year, related to the lunar calendar) during the daylight hours, and that they make a pilgrimage to Mecca. God was the God of the Jews but not a tribal God; He was the God of the Christians, but not a Trinity. Jesus was regarded only as a prophet, such as Mohammed, and not as the Son of God. There were no priests to intercede between believers and God, only "imams," or leaders, who called the faithful to prayer. Paradise was described as full of the good things of this world: wine, milk and honey, comforts and pleasures, "houris" (lovely maidens) to serve men and be their heavenly brides. Hell was a place of fire, hotter than the desert and containing all (and more) of the discomforts and sufferings of this world.

Hearing of Mohammed, the inhabitants of the city of Medina made a journey to Mecca and were converted to Mohammed's teachings. They invited him to take up his abode in Medina. When he learned that in Mecca there was a plot to murder him, he escaped with friends on swift camels. One friend remained in Mohammed's bed to fool his enemies who had surrounded his house. The flight, on the 16th of July, 622 CE, was called the Hegira. The Moslems reckon time from this date.

Mohammed was welcomed in Medina and became not only a spiritual but a political and military leader. Visions of Gabriel continued with revelations, and these were written down to become the Koran, the holy book of the Moslems.

The power and security Mohammed enjoyed changed him. His words and thoughts no longer sprang from a warm heart but from a cold intellect. He thought out everything beforehand to suit his purposes, no longer guided by the Spirit of God but by his own egotism. Islam, no longer a religion of peace and love, lost its gentleness and sense of the brotherhood of man. "Not to bring peace but a sword had he, the last and greatest of the prophets, appeared on earth." The struggle against the enemies of Islam was to be a sacred struggle. He who fell in the contest would pass, free from all sin and punishment, into

Paradise. No man need fear death as it was set by fate for each. If a man's hour had come, he could not escape it; if not, no danger could make it occur. The warlike Arabs rallied to such an appeal, and Mohammed became a leader of armies who went forth to subdue all unbelievers.

Mohammed first undertook to punish the Koreish people for driving him from their holy city. The Meccans were merchant princes, haughty and proud, looking down on the farmers of Medina. Mohammed easily won the support of the people of Medina, and they followed his leadership in waylaying the caravans of the Meccans, robbing them of the valuable wares that they were taking to Syria. One such expedition occurred during a sacred month when all warfare was supposed to be suspended. One of Mohammed's followers, at his command, fell upon a Koreish caravan and slew some of the men in charge of it. This deed aroused general indignation and Mohammed then proclaimed that war against the infidel was lawful at any period.

These raiding parties led to two important battles between the Meccans and the Medinians during which Mohammed marched into the field with his followers to fire their courage with prayers and promises of heavenly support. In both battles Mohammed's soldiers were outnumbered and yet they won.

After defeat, the Meccans withdrew to Mecca, content to guard the Kaaba and to prevent any Mohammedan from entering the holy city, or from taking part in any pilgrimage.

Next, Mohammed turned his forces against the Jews who lived around Medina and drove them out of their lands. The Jews then joined the Koreish and other Arab tribes and marched on Medina with an army of 10,000 men. Again Mohammed was outnumbered but cleverly defended the city by digging a trench around it. This strategy was successful in holding off the enemy long enough for him to sow mistrust and divisiveness among the enemy forces so that they withdrew after five weeks of siege in wintry weather. This withdrawal by the Arabs left the Jews alone to be overcome, and 700 Jewish men were then executed in the market place of Medina. The women and children were made slaves. The flocks and herds of the Jews were divided among the victors.

This victory was then inscribed in the Koran as a part of the Moslem scripture: "God drove the keepers of the Scriptures from their strong places and put fear in their hearts. One half of them he has slain; he has given you their lands, their dwellings, their goods, for an inheritance. God is almighty." More and more men flocked to Mohammed's cause, led by the greed for spoil as well as by hope of Paradise.

Now it was that Mohammed began to consider that Islam could and would spread to acquire the dominion of the world. Though the Jews had refused to recognize him as their Messiah, he felt that he could do without their homage if he could win the support of the Persians and the Christians. He sent messengers to Christians and Persian rulers, calling on them to worship the one true God who had revealed himself through Mohammed.

The Christians were expected to welcome him as a true prophet, for in the Koran he had related how Mary, after Gabriel had announced that she would bear a son, brought a child into the world under a palm tree, a child who had spoken even in the cradle, saying, "Truly I am a servant of Allah. He has given me the Book and has made me a prophet, And made me blessed wherever I may be—So peace be upon me the day I was born, the day I die, and the day I am raised alive!"

Several Christian princes and generals became converts to Islam, but the Persian ruler tore up the letter Mohammed had written him.

Mohammed's Arabs marched into Syria and had an encounter with Roman legions. This was successful, but not a final victory.

In 630 CE Mohammed marched against Mecca, knowing that if he could win it, all of Arabia would recognize him as its leader. By this time his forces were great. The people of Mecca were alarmed, one night, to see 10,000 watch fires burning on the mountains around the city, the watch fires of their now powerful enemy. One Meccan chief set out to reconnoiter, was captured and brought before Mohammed himself. As the Meccan had passed through the Moslem camp, he was so impressed with the size of it, with its banners, its weapons, soldiers armored in iron, and the devotion of these thousands to Mohammed, that he declared himself ready to honor the Prophet of God and to join the ranks of Islam. He was then released to return to Mecca, where he persuaded the Meccans to submit peacefully. The Moslem army then took possession of the city unresisted.

Enthroned in the holy city of Arabia as its prince and prophet after eight years of banishment, Mohammed now gave himself over to the noblest feelings and pardoned all his former enemies who immediately took up his standard. Then Mohammed went around the Kaaba seven times on his camel (an old act of worship), broke all the idols to pieces, but left the Black Stone untouched. Having thus purified the temple, he established it as the House of the Lord and issued a call to prayer from its rooftop.

It was not long before he subdued the surrounding hill tribes and destroyed their idols. After each new victory he was careful to see to it that his new converts among the vanquished received their share of the booty, whether it be in camels or in silver. When his old supporters complained about the favors he showered on but recent enemies, he said to them, "Be not angry if I seek to win the hearts of these with perishable goods. You shall share in Paradise with me." Whereupon the complainers wept, saying, "We are content with our lot."

Mecca now became the sacred city of the Moslems, as it had been for the heathen, with the Kaaba as a place of pilgrimage still sheltering the sacred stone of ancient days, supposedly the sign of God's favor toward the sons of Ishmael. Pilgrims swarmed to Mecca, to the Kaaba, to listen to the reading of the Koran and to its message that claimed:

- » no peace with any unbeliever,
- » no admission of any unbeliever into the temple, and
- » the perpetual war against unbelievers as the sacred duty of all Moslems.

From Syria to the south coast, from the Red Sea to the Persian Gulf, all tribes joined the faith in "the one God who has no fellow."

In the tenth year of the Hegira (632 CE), Mohammed marched at the head of a pilgrimage to Mecca followed by 114,000 followers. This pilgrimage became the pattern and example for all pilgrimages to Mecca in future times.

In the eleventh year of the Hegira, Mohammed was overtaken by a severe illness which lasted fourteen days. His mission on earth was completed, and as death approached him, he gave his slaves their freedom, ordered his money given to the poor, and then prayed, "God support me in the death struggle." His last words were, "I go to the glorious comrades in Paradise."

At the news of his death, a great wailing was raised and crowds gathered around his door in wild excitement. One of those close to Mohammed calmed the throng, saying,

> "O ye people, let him among you who served Mohammed know that Mohammed is dead, but let him who served God continue in His service, for Mohammed's God lives and never dies."

Three days later Mohammed's remains were lowered into the earth at the spot where he died. His tomb, along with the Kaaba, has remained till today a place of pilgrimage for all Moslems.

Passages from the Koran

(Translated from the Arabic by Arthur Jeffery, Heritage Press)

"The fact is, Allah is One. Allah is the Eternal.
He did not beget and He was not begotten,
And no one has ever been His peer."

This passage is very commonly used in the daily prayers, likely to be a rejection of the Christian teaching, for it was the Christians who spoke of the "only begotten Son," and put Jesus on a level with God.

***

"...for Allah's are the armies of heaven and earth, for Allah is knowing, wise; That He may make the believers, male and female, enter gardens between which rivers flow, wherein they are to abide eternally ... And that He may punish the hypocrites, male and female, the polytheists, male and female, who think evil with regard to Allah. For them is a circuit of evil, for Allah is angered with them and has cursed them, and has prepared Gehenna for them—how evil a destination! Allah's are the armies of the heavens and the earth, for Allah is sublime, wise."

***

"No blame rests on the blind, and no blame rests on the lame, and no blame rests on the sick for not responding to the call. Whoso obeys Allah and His messenger, him will He make enter gardens beneath which rivers flow, but whoso turns his back, him will He punish with a painful punishment. Allah was well-pleased with the believers ... And rewarded them with a speedy victory, And much spoils they might take, for Allah is sublime, wise. Allah promised you much spoils that ye might take ... But other spoils ye were not able to take, those Allah hath compassed, for Allah is powerful over every thing."

"The truth is from thy Lord, so on no account be thou among those who doubt. To each has been given a direction to which he turns in prayer. ... So from wherever thou has gone forth, turn thy face to the sacred shrine; and wheresoever ye Moslems may be, turn your faces toward it, that the people may have no argument against you, save those among them who do wrong. Do not fear them, fear Me; and do this that I may perfect My favour upon you, and may be ye will be guided. Accordingly We have sent among you a messenger from among yourselves to recite to your Our signs, and purify you, and teach you the Book and the Wisdom, and teach you what ye did not know. So remember Me, I shall remember you, and give thanks to Me, and be not ungrateful to Me.

"Verily, those who conceal the evidential signs and the guidance that We have sent down, after We have made it clear to the people in the Book, they are the ones Allah will curse, ... They, indeed, who disbelieve and die as infidels, they are those on whom is the curse of Allah, of the angels, and of the people altogether, under which they will be forever, their punishment never lightened for them, and having no expectancy of deliverance. Your God is One God, there is no Deity save Him, the Merciful, the Compassionate. ... Among the people are some who in place of Allah take substitutes which they love as one loves Allah. ... Could those who do wrong but see that Day when they will see the punishment, see that the power is wholly with Allah, and that Allah is severe in punishment. ... For them are in store sighings, but they will not get out from the Fire."

Holy Quran, National Museum, New Dehli

The Arabs Advance

Before Mohammed the Sons of Ishmael had been like the sands of their own desert: wild, scattered, easily blown by winds of love or hate, of hunger, of war; not as a rock united but in separate clans or tribes. Mohammed's life and message united them like a rock: solid and unscattered, held together by duty, faith, and the will to serve God.

Upon Mohammed's death, a near relative of his was elected by the faithful to be his successor, or *khalif*, and the khalif then became chief *imam* or interpreter of the Will of God. This he pronounced as the duty to win as many people to Islam as possible.

Driven by their warlike nature, their hopes of Paradise and their eagerness to do the Will of God, the Moslems began a conquest which extended eastward in the north and westward in the south, and in which they obeyed the word of the Koran by carrying war to all people who did not accept their faith.

The Roman Empire had failed; its outposts were weak and it was not hard for the vigorous Arabs to vanquish one people after another. Within a hundred years after the death of Mohammed, the Arabs had established an empire that included Arabia, Syria, Persia, Egypt, all of the northern coast of Africa, and even parts of India. But they could not capture Constantinople, the capital of what was now called the Byzantine Empire.

Everywhere else the Moslems marched from victory to victory, so feeble was the resistance. The more successes, the more desert tribesmen joined the conquerors in great waves of military might. "Arabia oozed forth her peoples." Jerusalem was conquered, Damascus, and the capital of Persia, and Alexandria in Egypt. The Atlas Mountains, parallel ranges with pleasant slopes and rich valleys, were easily taken all the way to Carthage.

Finding rich lands, better climate, and an easier life, the Arabs changed from being plunderers to colonists, settling down in their conquered lands. New colonizing expeditions followed the first warlike ones.

During these years, the Khalif saw to it that spoils were divided as the Prophet had decreed, one fifth to the Khalif at Medina and the remainder divided equally among the soldiers. But when it came to land, to avoid difficulties he ordered that the original owners had the right to their lands but, if they remained unbelievers, they must pay taxes to the Khalif. Conquered peoples were also permitted to retain their churches and synagogues but must cease ringing church bells, holding public processions, and praying aloud. Unbelievers could not ride in the presence of Moslems, might not wear the dress or arms of a Moslem, must abase themselves (take last place) and not look to have their word believed against that of a Moslem. The Arabs did not upset existing governments, as they did not know how to set up a new one. But their restrictions against unbelievers caused many to become converts and join their ranks.

The Khalifat, or Mohammedan capital, was moved from Medina to Damascus in 661 CE. Revenues from taxes rolled in to increase the wealth of the Khalifat, and as non-Arabs joined the faith, they too pushed out after new "spoils," like second waves pushed and stirred by the first. By the end of the century after Mohammed's death, the Arabian Empire extended along the eastern and southern coasts of the Mediterranean Sea, and the Moslems had become a seafaring power in command of the Sea.

The earliest of the conquerors had been the unlettered and uneducated adventurers from the deserts, the Arabs themselves. The later Moslems had a different background, more education, more culture and more civilized customs; but the Arabic language and religion became theirs.

In the Atlas Mountains lived a fair-skinned race, tall, bold, independent, yet akin to Arabs as horsemen, lancers, and fighters. They were the Berbers. The Greek "Ba-ba" meant a language Greeks could not understand, hence the word *barbarian*. The Berbers embraced Islam, even claiming to be the real descendants of Ishmael. The Eastern Moslems came to be called the Saracens (*Sarak* meaning East); and the Western Moslems were the Moors.

In 710 CE, north of the Mediterranean lay the broken remains of the Roman Empire, the original Romans and the Teutonic peoples both in decay, the one spoiled by luxury, the other by lawlessness. South of the Mediterranean the united new power of the Saracens and Moors was stirring, looking northward. A Saracen officer, Musa, was one who yearned to carry the faith of the Prophet into what he called the Isle of Andalusia, and he wrote a letter to the Khalif asking permission to do so, describing the beauties of that land in these words:

"It is Syria for the beauty of sky and soil; India for flowers and perfumes; Egypt for fruit; China for precious metals."

Then he sketched out a magnificent plan of conquest beginning with Spain and then passing through what is now France, Germany, and Hungary—and finally Constantinople.

He received permission. Musa's General was a Berber named Tariq (Tarik) who led 7,000 men across the strait between the Pillars of Hercules and landed in Spain on the rock since called Gibraltar (Jabal Tariq, the Mount of Tariq). Plundering the coast of Spain, Tariq met with Roderick's armies, defeated them, marched to Toledo and captured it. Musa followed with additional forces. Cordova, Seville, and all of Spain fell to the invaders and became part of the Moslem Empire. Roderick was said to have been killed in battle, while at the head of his troops, dressed in a helmet with horns of gold and a gown of beaten gold. Arab historians wrote, "Allah slew him by the hand of Tariq."

Tarik.

Arabism

To look into what the Arabs contributed to the world, let us picture the desert out of which they rode in such swarms as to overrun the world in less than 100 years. Two words paint the picture: sand and sun. The landscape was bare of plants and animals and the air was dry. *Bare, dry,* and *hard* are adjectives that can be added to the picture.

The tribesmen who made up the conquering armies had no culture, no civilization behind them. They were like uneducated children with the bodies of strong men. They did not know how to read or write. The bare, imageless desert inspired in them no art except poetry. Because of Mohammed's law forbidding the representation of animals or men, they looked with suspicion at images (idols) or decorations in the likeness of an elephant or other beast. But the poetry was chanted on all occasions, "camel chants" they were called, singing of the loading up of camels, the march, the trot, the halt at a water hole, just a few words endlessly repeated. Their only music was vocal with no harmony, just melody which was wailed in a coarse quality of voice, the melody drawn out like a thread, at times turning and twisting in very intricate patterns like a thin border of lacework along the edge of a garment. But they brought to other lands two novelties: their religion and their language.

Their language was rich and varied. This is a mystery, for from the desert tribes issued a language that was never at a loss for the right word and which, as it spread throughout the world, was adequate to express every meaning in the most cultured and thoughtful circles of other lands. How much clear thinking depends upon finding the right word! In a little more than a hundred years after the completion of the Arab conquests, their language had conquered even those whom their religion had not converted.

By the years 754–775, the khalif of the Moslem world was not so much a religious leader as he was an oriental tyrant who treated all men as his subjects. Al-Mansur moved the Khalifat from Damascus to the banks of the Tigris River, near the site of Babylon, where he built the wondrous city of Baghdad, chiefly of yellow brick, and where his palace was of such splendor as would have befitted the ancient Kings of Persia.

Now, just as the Khalifat was no longer in Arabia, so too the greater part of the Arab world was no longer in Arabia. What was left in Arabia did not undergo much change and is today quite like it used to be (except for the most recent cities resulting from the oil industry). What we speak of as the Arab civilization developed outside Arabia. Its people were not just the descendants of the earliest Arab invaders and colonists, but came to include many another race, as well as many another religious group. So, although the faith of Islam spread in many directions throughout the world and persists today in Pakistan, China, Africa, Turkey, Egypt, Iran, and so on, it did not capture the minds of thoughtful men. Wherever the Moslems went, they did not fail to meet men of learning and ability who refused to accept Islam even though they had to pay taxes and suffer discrimination. They scorned the idea that all knowledge was to be found in the Koran. The Moslems recognized that there was another realm to conquer, the realm of man's thoughts. Under the Khalifs of Baghdad, the Arabs began this new conquest.

In the city of Jundishapur, in southwestern Persia, the Arabs founded a center of Greek learning, the Academy of Jundishapur, where gathered many of the Greek scholars who had been driven out of the Roman Empire by Justinian. He had closed the mystery schools of Athens and banished all teachers who were connected with Hellenistic learning. Scholars from Persia and India had also gathered at Jundishapur to pursue their studies: philosophers, astronomers, mathematicians, and medical scientists. Here, among other collections to be found were the writings of Plator and Aristotle. Strangely, what was left to the world of Greek culture had been preserved in Persia, the ancient enemy of Greece.

A hundred years after the time of Julian the Apostate, a Syrian Christian named Nestorius questioned the Divinity of Christ, claiming for Him only one nature—human—and not two—human and Divine. He argued that being the "Son of God" he must have been younger than the Father, must have been a "creature" rather than "Creator." Those who followed this belief withdrew from the Church in the West and were henceforth called Nestorian Christians, and it was in Jundishapur that the Nestorians were at work as the leading scholars of Greek thought. In Jundishapur, as well as in Alexandria and other eastern cities, the Arabs found the capitals of that learning which they must win in order to be fit rulers of the world.

The Baghdad Khalifs, Harun al-Rashid among them, decided that such books as were to be found in Jundishapur and elsewhere must be translated into Arabic if they were to benefit the Arabs.

Harun al-Rashid, Khalif from 786–809 CE, succeeded his brother Muss al-Hadi, the fourth Khalif, a year after the death of his father Mahdi, the third Khalif. In his youth, Harun had been very successful as a general in invasions of Asia Minor. His empire came to include all southwestern Asia and northern Africa. He had diplomatic relations with Charlemagne, the Frankish King in Europe, and with China. His prime minister was Fazl ibn Rabi. Harun was a munificent patron of letters and the arts, and under him Baghdad was at its apogee. He became a great figure for the Arabs who tell many of the stories of the Thousand and One Nights about him.   – Columbia Encyclopedia

Harun al-Rashid

Aristotle's books were translated by the Nestorians into Syriac (the Syrian language). Now the Khalif gave the task of translating Greek philosophy and science into Arabic to men of learning who were not Moslems: some were Jews, others were Persians, some were Christians, and some were Sabians (wise men of Saba). The Arab nobles around the court of the Khalif vied with each other in collecting books. Within the next hundred years, Aristotle, Plato, Ptolemy, Hippocrates, Galen, Euclid, and Archimedes were translated into Arabic, all having to do with science and philosophy. None of the poetry, drama, or history of Greece was touched; it was passed by. Their interest was in science and mathematics.

The Khalif al-Mamum (831–833 CE), the successor of al-Rashid, founded a school for the study of Greek science and philosophy in

Harun al-Ma'mūn

31

Baghdad, and it was called the "House of Wisdom." The leading scholar in this school was Hunain, a Nestorian physician who, with his pupils, carried forward the translations and studies of Greek culture. The Khalif sent out men to Egypt and Syria to find and bring back manuscripts as yet untranslated. Thus was formed, in Baghdad, one of the greatest libraries in the world for the benefit of Moslems. Remaining scholars and translators in Jundishapur were transferred to Baghdad and the famous Academy disappeared.

Not having any science or philosophy of their own, the Arabs finally captured what the Greeks had developed, as well as Hindu and Persian mathematics and astronomy. They now pursued learning with vigor, making their own studies and writing many books; but in all their work they had to start with the work of someone else. Arab culture came to be a gathering together of many cultures, only in the realm of the mind.

Among their scholars were:

- » al Kindi, called the first Arab philosopher because he made a study of Aristotle and wrote a book about Aristotle's system of logic.
- » al Kwarizmi, who wrote a book entitled *Algebra* (825 CE) based on a combination of Greek and Hindu mathematics. The term *algorithm* is derived from his name. He introduced the use of 0 (zero) for the first time, a Hindu practice. Previously the Greeks and Romans had to count with the abacus and had no "zero." Now, with the zero and the written Arabic numbers, the decimal system and number places were devised.

9 8 7 6 Y Z Σ 6 I O

- » The poet Omar Khayam was also an astronomer. He developed a more perfect calendar. The Khalif al-Mamun erected an observatory in Baghdad, and Arab astronomers working there developed a more perfect astrolabe from that used by the Greeks and a better compass than the crude needle of the Chinese.
- » In medicine, Rhazes brought together into one book, called *The Comprehensive Book*, the knowledge and treatment for every disease known by Greeks, Arabs, Persians, and Indians.

Other sciences furthered by Arab scholars were geography, physics, chemistry, meteorology, and engineering. Thus did the Arabs conquer the mind of the world by studying it, for the most part like students of what they found and not creating in themselves anything new.

One of the last and greatest Arab thinkers was a Spanish Moslem named Averroes. He was a doctor and lawyer, and he wrote a commentary on Aristotle, interpreting the philosopher as claiming that the immortal soul and the world soul (*anima mundi*) were the same (a principle that denies human individuality), and that what is true in the light of faith may be untrue in the eyes of reason (the beginning of the conflict between faith and reason…).

In conclusion, perhaps the best picture of Arabism is that of an Arab house with its screens and walls decorated with delicately interweaving designs, traceries in grill work, and mosaics, like the melodies of the "camel chants."

Astrolabe

Illustration by Albert Letchford in *A Thousand and One Arabian Nights*, "Tale of the Tailor" — "So I bade the page open the box and the Barber laid down the astrolabe; and, sitting on the ground, turned over the scents and incense and aloes-wood and essences till I was well-nigh distraught."

The Religion of the Crescent

(Notes from Background to the Gospel of St. Mark, Lecture Nine, by Rudolf Steiner)

When we try to form some conception of how…the Christ-idea arose out of thoughts and feelings of the immediately preceding period, we must remember that the Jahve—or Jehovah—idea meant as much to the ancient Hebrews as the Christ-idea meant to those who became his followers. …We must understand clearly that there is an intimate relationship between the Jahve-idea and the Christ-idea… I need only remind you again of the picture of the sunlight which can come to us either directly from the Sun or by reflection at night from the Moon, especially at full moon. If we think of Christ as symbolized by the direct sunlight, we may liken Jahve to sunlight reflected by the Moon and that would represent the exact sense in which the two ideas should be understood. … Jahve is an indirect and Christ a direct revelation of the same Being.

If we call the religion of Christ a Sun-religion …we may call the Jahve-religion a Moon-religion, the transitory reflection of the Christ-religion. Thus in a period preceding the birth of Christianity, the Sun-religion was prepared for by a Moon-religion. … Symbols are not chosen arbitrarily but have deep foundations. When a world conception or world-religion is associated with a symbol, those who use the symbol with adequate knowledge are aware that it is intimately and essentially connected with what it represents.

Conditions present in pre-Christian times during the period of ancient Hebrew culture reappeared later in post-Christian times: Something that was prepared within the Jahve-religion, overlapping the Christ Impulse as it were, appeared again and played into the other factors which had by then developed.

Taking the Moon, contrasted with the Sun, as the symbol representing the Jahve-religion, we may expect that a similar form of belief, bypassing as it were the Christ Impulse, would emerge later on as a kind of Moon-religion. And this is what actually happened. The old Jahve-religion emerged again after the Christ Event, in the religion of the Crescent, carrying earlier impulses into post-Christian times. … So in a later time we have the repetition of an earlier phase that has skipped the intervening years. … Beginning in the sixth century CE and exercising a very vigorous influence upon all aspects of development, we have the religion brought by the Arabians from Africa over into Spain. This represents a re-emergence, in a different form, of the Jahve-Moon-religion. The intervening Christ Impulse has been ignored … disregarded in the religion of Islam which was actually a kind of revival of Mosaic monotheism.

Something that had passed as it were through a filter was thus brought into Europe by the Arabians. Old concepts… were denuded of their visionary, pictorial content and recast into abstract forms. They reappear in the wonderful scientific knowledge possessed by the Arabians who made their way into Europe via Africa and Spain. Whereas Christianity brought an impulse connected essentially with man's life of soul, the greatest impulse given to the human intellect was brought by the Arabians.

Only through the union of Christianity and Mohammedanism …was it possible for our modern culture to come into being.

The Early Middle Ages

More about the Franks

When the Moslems, in the course of their conquests, moved from Spain over the Pyrenees into Gaul, they came face to face with the Franks, who by this time occupied all of Gaul and lands to the west of Gaul, north of Italy. In their first skirmishes across the border, the Moors were successful, and a large army of them began an invasion intended as a conquest of Europe.

In 732 CE the Moslems approached Tours, a rich city of one of the Frankish kingdoms. In the long centuries of conflict between the peoples of the East and of the West, the Easterners had never come so close to winning the West. If it hadn't been for a Frankish army led by a general named Charles Martel (the Hammer, so named after this victory), the whole history of the world would have been different. He stopped the Moors. After their defeat they withdrew to Spain, where they remained for many years and developed a great and prosperous kingdom.

Charles Martel was the Mayor of the Palace of the Frankish King of Neustria. Other Frankish kingdoms in Gaul—Austrasia, Alemania, Bavaria, Burgundy, Aquitania, Gascony, and Provincia, together with Neustria—were brought together as one by a Frankish king named Clovis but, after his death in 511 CE, the various kingdoms became divided again. However, Clovis brought another kind of unity into the stream of European history. He had a Christian wife, and through her influence he too became, at least in name, a Christian. Before battle he prayed for the help of Jesus Christ, promising to be baptized if victorious. Thus he became a Christian and had his army also baptized, but, in spite of this, he remained cruel, ruthless, and half-civilized.

During the next 200 years, inequalities developed between classes of men, between the kings, their vassals, and their serfs. The weak, luxury-loving rulers were termed the "Do Nothings" (Fainéants).

Pepin the Short
(from Harold Lamb's *Charlemagne*)

The son of Charles Martel, Pepin the Short succeeded his father as Master (mayor) of the Palace of Childerich III, one of the Do Nothing Kings. "Pepin carried out the actual task of ruling with a hard, quick hand, while the King had merely come forth from his homestead, riding in the ritual cart drawn by plodding oxen, driven by a long-haired peasant, to the assembly each year. There the fat drone had faced the gathering of his folk and had given his consent to the things they had done or wished to do."

Pepin, having the real power and the ability to use it, sent a messenger to Rome to ask a question of the Pope: "Should not he who holds the power in a kingdom have the title as well?"

The Pope's answer was, "It seems better that he who has power in the state should be the king, and be called King, rather than he who is falsely called King." That is why Childerich III was then led out not to the year's assembly but to a monastery in the forest. He was driven away in his ox cart, "from his farm and cooks and women, to have his fine red hair shaved off like a monk."

The assembly lifted Pepin up on their shields and hailed him as king. Bishop Boniface, the Pope's Apostle to the Germans, anointed him with holy oil and set a crown of gold on his head.

From now on the King (chieftain) was no longer selected by the other warriors for his bravery but appointed by the Pope as "the Lord's Anointed." The Pope threatened with God's anger anyone who should attempt to overthrow the consecrated family of Pepin. Thus it became a religious duty to obey the king, regarded by the Church as God's representative on earth, "King by the Grace of God," against whom it was a sin to revolt, no matter how bad he might be.

> *Charlemagne, one of the greatest men of all time,*
> *stands at the end of one age and at the beginning of another,*
> *and what he did was the foundation of all the future history*
> *of Europe.* – E. Emerton, Professor of History, Harvard, 1892

Charlemagne
Caroli Magni (742–814 CE) Charles the Great

The son of Pepin the Short, Charlemagne managed toward the end of his life to unite all of Western Europe, except Spain and southern Italy, into a single Christian community.

As a person he was fit to be a leader toward a future time, for he did not bear in his nature merely the customs and habits of his Frankish predecessors who imposed their tribal ways on the people they conquered. The fire of the old Roman civilization had died out. The Arabs had captured the southern half of the empire. The Christian Church was established in Rome, and Christian knights and saints and monks were working in England among the "heathen" Angles and Saxons.

Like other German tribes, the Franks could neither read nor write and had little knowledge of world history. They were content with their own strength and with the way in which this strength won for them the material comforts of good lands, houses, animals, food, drink, and clothing. As they were a strong people, the Roman Church recognized that to win them over would be a means of strengthening its influence. Thus it was that Charles, son of Pepin, came to be crowned by the Pope himself as Emperor of a new Roman empire, "The Holy Roman Empire."

As a boy of eleven years, Charles was "over-tall and gangling, yet with a spread to his shoulders and wide bones in his hands that marked him for strength." His dark hair was cropped close and "his voice came shrill" from his clumsy body. His father made him stay beside him from morning to noon listening to the appeals and complaints that were brought to the King by his people. His mother made him study with the deacons who taught the boys in the Palace School.

He was taught the "science of numbers":
Question: "If you gathered 30 chestnuts and ate five each day, how many days of the week would the chestnuts last?"
Answer: "Until the Lord's day of rest."

He was taught "the science of physical things":
Question: "What is light?"
Answer: "The torch that reveals everything."

All that the boys needed to learn were the answers to the questions. They learned to read from the Old Testament, reading aloud the stories of Saul and Sodom and so on. It seemed to Charles that the answers and the miraculous happenings in the books had nothing to do with the troubles and sufferings of the human beings who approached his father.

In addition Charles was trained to use weapons: sword and shield, lance of ash wood, and scramasax (a heavy, curved knife). "Being long of limb, the boy could grasp his horse fast with his legs, and keep his shield out of the way of his horse well enough; but he was too clumsy to hurl the six-foot lance fairly, at a gallop, into the target."

Charles felt at home in the forest. He could follow deer tracks through the thickest oak groves, see the swift change in shadows that marked a panther stealing away, recognize the faint signs of a feeding bear. He kept his direction by instinct, certain of finding his way out. If he chose to sleep through a night in the forest, he could find a stream and make a fire.

Now here was a boy, slow in studies, clumsy of body, strong in his sense for the wildness of nature—and he was to become a great leader of men, who:

» established schools for children,
» formed a systematic government,
» won many a battle over neighboring enemies, the Saxons in the north, the Moors in the south, so as to unite a large territory under his rule, which began when he was 26 years old in 768 CE,
» became a devoted Christian and required that those he conquered be baptized, and saw to it that a great cathedral was built in Aix-la-Chapelle-Aachen where his subjects could worship as Christians, and
» was finally made Emperor by the Pope, on Christmas Day, in St. Peter's Church in Rome, in the year 800.

What brought out the qualities in his nature that made him a builder of society? There was one man who inspired Charles more than any other.

After he became king, Charles met with a learned Celt named Alcuin who as a scholar was trained in a church school in England. Alcuin, through Charlemagne, did more than anyone else to inspire the revival of learning in 9th-century Europe. He wrote books on religion and on grammar and organized Charlemagne's Palace School and established other schools in the Frankish kingdom.

Charlemagne met Alcuin in Parma, Italy, where in a monastery Alcuin was in bed with a fever. On a pilgrimage to Italy he was taken with the fever "caught in the marshes of Rome." The story of their meeting is that the "45-year-old Briton rose up from a bed of fever to greet Charlemagne with high good humor."

Charles: Why did you rise to greet me?
Alcuin: I saw Your Excellence walking where you did not exist.

Charles: How?
Alcuin: (pointing to a pool of water in the courtyard) I saw your image in the water.

Charles: How did you understand who I was?
Alcuin: Who else would walk alone before all others?

It was then, after further conversation, that Charlemagne persuaded Alcuin to be the schoolmaster for the children of the Palace in Aachen. But Alcuin was to be more than a teacher of the children. He was to become the teacher of Charlemagne.

Charles began to realize how dark and dull were the minds of the Franks, whose only thoughts were of loyalty to their king, when he was confronted with the thoughtfulness of Alcuin, who taught him, "Memory is the power of the mind which recalls the past. Intelligence is the power to understand the present. Foresight is the power to perceive what will come to pass."

Humbly, Charles reflected that he had a good memory to start with, for he could remember the stories of his forebears, including those of Arnulf, the first of his family, who had thrown his seal ring into the River Seine, saying that if the ring came back to him, he would rule over his fellow men. After years passed, a fish was cut open on Arnulf's table and his ring fell out. And now, himself the ruler of the entire Frankish kingdom, Charles hoped that, by degrees and constant labor, he might gain some intelligence.

Having little time during the day, Charles practiced writing with his clumsy fingers at night by candlelight. He always found it easy to learn what he could hear, but very difficult to learn by reading, where the interwoven letters were hard to connect with meaning. Because of these, his own weaknesses, he became determined that the children in his kingdom should learn to write and read. He called on Alcuin to start schools in other parts of his kingdom, and the one in Tours became one of the best.

Aachen was the city wherein Charlemagne maintained his capital. Here it was that he supervised the building of the beautiful cathedral that represented his allegiance to the Christian faith. And from this city he ruled the territories he had conquered as a leader of brave knights and companions.

He divided his domain into districts called counties, governed by counts in his name. The counts had to keep order in their counties, raise troops when Charlemagne needed them, and act as judges when disputes and quarrels arose. He sent out inspectors in pairs, one of whom was always a churchman, to see if the counts were in need of help and to keep the King informed of what was going on in the counties.

At length, the Pope recognized the strength and purpose that Charles had shown as King of Frankland and crowned him as "Emperor of the Romans," although the Romans had long since disappeared from the pages of history.

Of his coronation it is told that, wearing a Roman tunic, chlamys, and sandals of a Roman patrician (at the Pope's behest), Charles entered St. Peter's Church in Rome. A thousand candles glowed. The church bells rang and echoed. The church was crowded with priests, with the bishops of Frankland, and with the nobles of Rome. Charlemagne knelt to pray before the statues of the saints and angels above the tomb of St. Peter. As he rose from his prayers, Pope Leo came to him and placed a crown on his head. The candle glow flickered in tiny lights from the jewels in the crown. Voices shouted in chorus, "To Charles, Augustus, crowned by God, great and peace-giving Roman Emperor, long life and victory!" Twice was the chorus repeated. Then the Pope, with his attendants, clothed Charlemagne with a purple mantle and knelt down before him as if to a Caesar, an Augustus, and the word *imperator* was pronounced at the end of the ceremonies.

It is also told that when Charlemagne entered St. Peter's Church, he did not expect all that was to happen. He had come there to worship and had worn the garments of a Roman patrician in reverence for the Pope. And when he had been crowned as Emperor, as an Augustus, he said, "If I had known what Leo meant to do, I would never have set foot in this church, even on this Christmas Day."

Charlemagne's Conquests

Through the crowning of Charlemagne as Emperor of the former Roman lands in the West, the Church (Pope) was able to claim more power for itself. Charlemagne had already taken under his rule many of his Teutonic neighbors who had taken possession of a large part of Italy. Then there were the Saxons who still came in waves from the north seeking new lands in the south. And in the south, in Spain, were the Moors who continued to try to win their way into northern regions.

Certain old stories of these times have come down to us by way of monks, Frankish historians, and other storytellers. One such story concerns the Lombard King Desiderius. During the years 773–774, the Pope had called upon Charles to subdue Desiderius and Charles crossed the Alps. Now Desiderius had had success in winning the weakened inhabitants of Italy, but he was afraid of the Frankish warriors led by Charles and shut himself up within the walls of Pavia, the Lombard capital, due north of Corsica, and was besieged by the Franks. An old chronicle tells us:

> As the King (Charles) drew near, there flashed upon the besieged a day that was more terrible for them than any night. They saw him, Karl, the man of steel, his arms covered with plates of steel, his iron breast and his broad shoulders protected by a steel harness; his left hand carried aloft the iron lance, for his right was always ready for the victorious steel. His thighs, which others leave uncovered in order the more easily to mount their horses, were covered on the outside with iron scales. This armor all who rode before him, beside him, or who followed him, had tried to imitate as closely as possible. Steel

filled the fields and roads. The rays of the sun were reflected from the gleaming steel. The people, paralyzed by fear, did homage to the bristling steel. The fear of the gleaming steel pierced down deep into the earth. "Alas, the steel! Alas, the steel!" resounded the confused cries of the inhabitants…And the courage of youths fled before the steel.

Desiderius made little resistance and surrendered the city and his crown to Charles, who did not try to make Lombardy part of the Frankish kingdom, but rather made himself King of the Lombards. The Lombard government was not disturbed. The only change was that whereas before the nobility had had Desiderius as their overlord, they now had Charles, the King of the Franks. The common people probably had no idea as to who their sovereign might be.

Charles's wars with the Saxons lasted, on and off, for 30 years (772–803). These were the people who sent invading warriors into England and who tried to prove the mettle of the new King of the Franks in various small attacks, over the lowlands, against the Frankish settlements beyond the Rhine. The stories of Charles's victories over the Saxons have a different mood and quality. Some of these stories were:

Charles led an army against a Saxon fortress and destroyed the trunk of a tree that was sacred to the people. This led the people to beg for peace and to promise to abide by the terms laid down by the conquerer.

Just after capturing another Saxon stronghold (Eresburg), the Frankish army was driven to desperation by thirst when, suddenly, a stream of water burst out of the ground to relieve their thirst and suffering.

When the Saxons advanced against a Frankish garrison to burn the building, a church in which the Franks had taken refuge, they saw two angels clothed in white floating in the air above the church and fled in terror to their woods. When the Franks came out of the church, they found, kneeling close to the building, a Saxon struck lifeless in the act of holding a torch as he attempted to set fire to the church.

Great numbers of Saxon youths, taken as prisoners, were sent to various monasteries in Frankland to be instructed in Christian ways and the arts of civilization. They, together with the victories won by Charles's armies, helped to persuade the Saxons to take up the Frankish and Christian way of life.

The northern part of Spain, for generations under the control of the Visigoths, had been conquered by the Moslems. Charlemagne set out to free these Gothic people from their "heathen" rulers. He led a great army southward, about the year 812 and after he was crowned Emperor, beyond the Ebro River to a Moorish stronghold, Saragossa. He met with little resistance, then returned northward, leaving his rear guards behind as he established Frankish garrisons between the Ebro and the Pyrenees.

At the Pass of Roncesvalles a rear guard was attacked by the Moors, and Roland, one of Charlemagne's counts, was slain. The courage and the death of Roland became a legend that epitomized the struggle between the Christians and the Moors.

The permanent result of Charlemagne's Spanish expedition was that the whole of northern Spain came under his rule. It was the beginning of "recovering the soil of Spain from the hated Moor" on into the 15th century and ending with the conquest of Granada.

The Song of Roland

(Excerpts from translation by Merriam Sherwood, for dramatic recitation)

(Throughout the presentation the whole cast of characters may remain on stage, reciting the narrative parts together, moving to various parts of the stage to indicate change of scene. Individual characters step forward to enact the dialogues.)

SCENE 1

Narrative: King Charles, our mighty Emperor, had been full seven years in Spain. Even to the seaboard he had conquered that high land. No castle could stand before him. Wall nor city remained to be battered down, save only Saragossa which is upon a mountain. King Marsile held it, a king who loved not God. Evil needs must overtake him.

The Emperor was in a great orchard. With him were Roland and Oliver, Duke Samson and Anseis the Proud, Geoffrey of Anjou, the King's Standard-Bearer. With these many others, fifteen thousand in all, from sweet France. The knights were sitting on white carpets. Under a pine tree, beside an eglantine, a throne, all of pure gold, had been set up. There sat the King who ruled sweet France. White was his beard and hoary his head: noble his figure and proud his bearing.

Some messengers dismounted and gave him greetings of love and good will.

Blancandrin: God save you, God the Glorious, whom we should adore! This message we bring you from King Marsile the Noble. He would give you largely of his wealth: bears and lions and greyhounds on the leash, seven hundred camels and a thousand molted falcons, four hundred mules laden with gold and silver, fifty thousand wains to carry it away. You have been in this country long enough. It is time you returned to Aix in France. When you are in the royal palace, at the great feast of St. Michael of the Peril of the Sea, my liege lord will follow you there, so he says. In your baths, made there for you by God, would he be made a Christian.

Charles: Fair is your speech. Nevertheless, King Marsile is very much my enemy!

The French:	It behooves us to beware.
Roland:	Woe the day you trust Marsile!
Ganelon:	Woe the day you trust a poltroon! When King Marsile sends to you, saying that he will become your vassal, hands clasped, and that he will hold all Spain as a gift from you; nay further that he will receive the faith that we hold: whoever counsels you to reject this offer cares not, Sire, what death we die.
Naimes:	You have just heard the answer of Count Ganelon. Wisdom contains it; then listen to it.
The French:	The Duke hath spoken well.
Charles:	Noble Lords, whom shall we send to Saragossa, to King Marsile?
Naimes:	I will go, with your permission.
Charles:	You are a sage. By this beard and by my mustache, you shall not go at this time so far from me. Go take your seat. No one is calling upon you! Noble Lords, whom can we send to the Saracen who holds Saragossa?
Roland:	I am the one to go.
Oliver:	Certainly not! Your temper is short and your disposition proud. I should be afraid that you would get into trouble. If the King so wishes, I might well be sent.
Charles:	Be quiet, both of you! Neither you nor Roland shall take your feet thither. Noble Knights, choose for me a baron of my land to bear my message to Marsile.
Roland:	Send Ganelon, my stepfather.
The French:	He is indeed the one. If you choose not him, you will not send a wiser.
Ganelon:	(to Roland) Utter fool! Whence thy madness? It is well-known that I am thy stepfather, yet thou hast picked me. If God grant that I return thence, such misfortune will I bring upon thee as shall last out thy lifetime!
Charles:	Your anger is too great. Certainly you will go since I command it.
Ganelon:	My Lords, you will hear from this!

SCENE 2

Narrative: In the shade of a pine tree stood a throne draped in silk of Alexandria. There, surrounded by twenty thousand Saracens, sat the King who held all Spain.

Behold Ganelon and Blancandrin! Blancandrin came before Marsile, hand in hand with Count Ganelon.

Ganelon: God save you, God the Glorious, whom we should adore! Charlemagne the Noble sends you this message: You must accept holy Christianity. Half of Spain he will give you in fief. His nephew Roland shall have the other half. In him you will have a haughty fellow vassal. If you will not agree to this, the Emperor will come to besiege you in Saragossa.

Marsile: I marvel at Charlemagne, who is white-haired and old. I think he is two hundred years old and more. His body has toiled in so many lands, he has borne so many blows of lances and spears, has brought to beggary so many rich kings. When will he abandon making war?

Ganelon: Never as long as Roland lives! There is none so valiant from here to the orient under the tent of the sky. Very brave also is his comrade Oliver; and the Twelve Peers, whom Charles holds so dear, form the Emperor's vanguard with twenty thousand Franks. Safe is Charles, nor fears he living man.

Marsile: Fair Sir Ganelon, I can raise an army of four hundred thousand knights. How can I compass Roland's death?

Ganelon: Give the Emperor so much of your wealth that all the French shall marvel at it. If you send him twenty hostages, the King will return to sweet France, leaving his rear guard behind him. In that, I believe, will be his nephew, Count Roland, and Oliver the Brave and Courtly. Twenty thousand Frenchmen they have in their company. Send against them 100,000 of your Pagans to offer battle to the rear guard. Dead men are the counts if you follow my advice. Charles will see his great pride fallen. He will never again wish to make war on you. He who might compass the death of Roland would cause Charles to lose his right arm from his body. His glorious armies would take the field no more.

Narrative:	When Marsile heard this, he kissed Ganelon's neck; then commanded that his treasure be brought.
Marsile:	What further shall I say? You shall pledge me your word to betray Roland.
Ganelon:	Let it be as you wish.
Narrative:	On the relics in his sword, Murgleis, he swore the treason, and thus he did do wrong.

SCENE 3

Narrative:	The Emperor had risen early. He had heard Mass and Matins, and was standing on the green grass before his tent. Roland was there and Oliver the Brave, Duke Naimes and many others. There came Ganelon, the Wicked, the Foresworn.
Ganelon:	God save you! I bring you here the keys of Saragossa, and I have fetched enormous riches for you, and twenty hostages. As for the Pagan king, Sire, you may rest assured that you will not see this first month pass before he follows you to France, where he will receive the faith that you profess and, with his hands clasped, become your vassal, to hold the kingdom of Spain for you.
Charles:	God be praised! You have done well and you will not be the loser thereby.
Narrative:	A thousand trumpets were blown throughout the host. The French broke camp, and had their pack-horses loaded. The Emperor rode proudly through the army.
Charles:	Noble Lords, behold the pass and the narrow defiles! Choose for me, pray, the leader of the rear guard.
Ganelon:	Let it be my stepson, Roland. No other baron have you of such prowess.
Roland:	Sir Stepfather, I have cause to love you well since you have named me for the rear guard. Charles, the King who holds France, will, methinks, lose thereby neither palfrey nor charger, neither mule nor ass, nor saddle horse nor sumpter, without it be purchased first by the sword.

Charles:	Fair Sir Nephew, know forsooth that I will leave you half my army. Take them. They will be your salvation.
Roland:	That I will not do. God confound me if I disgrace my lineage thus. Twenty thousand valiant Franks will I retain. You may cross the pass with entire confidence. Woe the day you fear any man as long as I am living!
Narrative:	High were the peaks and shadowy the vales, black the rocks and monstrous the defiles. That day the French passed dolorous. For fifteen leagues the noise of their marching could be heard. More than all the rest Charlemagne was filled with anguish. Had he not left his nephew at the pass into Spain?

SCENE 4

Narrative:	Fair was the day and bright the sun. A thousand trumpets blew, to make it fairer still. So loud was the sound that the French heard it.
Oliver:	Sir Comrade, methinks we may have battle with the Saracens.
Roland:	God grant that it be so!
Oliver:	What a clamor I perceive coming from Spain. How many hauberks gleaming white, how many flaming helmets! The Pagans have come in great force. We French are very few. Roland, my comrade, blow your horn. Charles will hear it, and the army will return.
Roland:	That were the act of a fool! I should lose thereby my renown in sweet France. Woe to the faithless Pagans who have come to the pass! I swear to you, they are all destined to die!
Oliver:	Roland, my comrade, blow your horn! Charles will hear it and will lead the army back. The King and his barons will succor us.
Roland:	God forbid that my kin should be blamed because of me, or that sweet France should fall into disgrace. Woe to the faithless Pagans here assembled. I swear to you, they shall be slain.
Oliver:	Roland, my comrade, blow your horn! Charles will hear it as he crosses the pass. I swear to you the Franks will return.

Roland:	God forbid that it be said by any living man that for fear of Pagans I blew my horn. Sir Comrade, Friend, cease your complaints. Smite with thy lance, as I with Durandel, my good sword, which the King gave me. If I die, he who wins it can say: "This was the sword of a noble vassal!"
Narrative:	Roland was bold and Oliver was wise. Both were of surpassing courage. Never for fear of death would they shun battle. Roland crossed the pass of Spain on his swift horse. He bore his arms. Which became him well, and rode, brandishing his spear, the point toward heaven, the white pennant floating at the tip, with its fringes of gold beating against his hands. Noble was his figure, his face bright and laughing. His comrade, Oliver, followed closely behind him.
Roland:	Noble Lords, ride softly, slowly! Today we shall win booty fair and noble. No king of France had ever spoils so rich.
Oliver:	Noble Lords, stand your ground! In God's name I pray you, give all your thought to dealing blows. As you receive them, give them back. Nor let us forget the battle cry of Charles!
Narrative:	At these words the French gave the battle cry. Montjoie! They dug the spurs into their horses urging them to greater speed. The Saracens received them fearlessly. Franks and Pagans—behold the fight engaged!
	Prodigious was the battle; not a man but fought. Count Roland took no thought for his safety. He thrust with his spear as long as the shaft remained. He drew his naked sword, Durandel, that cut and carved well. He made a great slaughter of the Saracens. Oliver rode through the melee. His lance was broken, only the stump remained. My Lord Oliver drew his good sword and showed that he could wield it as a knight should.
Roland:	I recognize you, Brother, in that blow! 'Tis for buffets like that that the Emperor loves us.
The French:	Montjoie!
Narrative:	Marvelous and mighty was the battle. The French smote with their burnished spears. How great the suffering you might have seen there! How many men dead and wounded and bleeding. They lay one upon the other, on their backs and on their faces.

SCENE 5

Narrative: Oliver felt himself wounded to the death. He lost his sense of hearing and of sight. He dismounted and lay on the ground. He confessed his sins in a loud voice, both hands clasped toward heaven, and prayed to God to grant him Paradise and to bless Charles and sweet France and, above all, his comrade Roland. His heart failed, his helmet sank, his whole body fell upon the ground. Dead was the Count, no longer might he live.

Roland: Sir Comrade, alas for your bold courage! We have been together for years and for days. You have never done me harm, nor I you. Since you are dead, it is my grief that I live.

Narrative: With these words did Roland faint upon his horse. He was held on by his stirrups of fine gold; thus wheresoever he might go, he could not fall off.

Before Roland came to himself, a great disaster befell him: the French were slain; he had lost them all.

Four hundred Pagans assembled from among those who deemed themselves best in the field. Hard and heavy the attack they made of Roland. When Count Roland saw them advancing, how strong and fierce and eager he became. He would not yield to them as long as life remained. He sat his horse. He dug in his spurs of fine gold, and rode to attack them all in the thick of the press.

The Pagans said, "Alack that we were ever born. Dire for us the day that dawned this morning. We have lost our lords and peers. So fierce and proud is Count Roland that he will never be vanquished by mortal man. Let us take aim at him and leave it at that."

They cast at him a bevy of spears and lances and feathered darts. Then the Pagans fled and left Roland there. The pagans fled angry and wrathful. They made every effort to return toward Spain.

Roland felt that death was taking hold of him. From his head it was descending toward his heart. Beneath a pine tree he went running. He lay down on his face on the green grass. Under him he placed his sword and horn. He turned his head toward the Pagan people. This he did so that all men should say that he, the gentle Count, died conquering.

	He began to mind him of many things: of how many lands he had conquered, of sweet France, of the men of his kin, of Charlemagne his Lord who had fostered him. He could not but weep and sigh. He confessed his sins and prayed God for mercy.
Roland:	True Father, Who never liest, Thou Who didst raise Lazarus from the dead, and save Daniel from the lions, keep, I pray Thee, my soul from all perils arising from the sins I have committed in my life.
Narrative:	He offered his right glove to God. Saint Gabriel took it from his hand. On his arm his head was resting. With clasped hands he went to his death. God sent to him His angel Cherubim and St. Michael of the Peril of the Sea. St. Gabriel came with them. Together they bore the soul of the Count to Paradise.

Frontispiece by Léon Gautier (1832–1897) to *La Chanson de Roland*, 11e édition. Public domain

The Age of Disorder

Charlemagne died in the year 814. His son, Louis the Pious, tried to share his estates and lands between his brothers in a peaceful manner, but that did not prevent them from quarreling, each one thinking of how much was due him. After Louis' death they continued the fight, and what had been united as one empire by Charlemagne was now divided into three kingdoms: the Western Frankish and the Eastern Frankish Kingdoms and the Kingdom of Italy. All that Charlemagne had attempted to establish order and civilization was now caught up in confusion and disorder that lasted for the next two to three hundred years.

Now the question was not, "Which King will gain the greatest power in Europe?" The question of power, and the struggle to win the supreme authority in human affairs, arose in quite another way—between the kingdoms of this world and "the kingdom of heaven," between the landowners and the Church.

THE MEDIEVAL CASTLE and THE MONASTERY

The great lords of the land dwelt in castles built of stone, usually high upon some rock cliff overlooking miles of the surrounding country. The walls of the castle were ten to twenty feet thick and a hundred or more feet high. Round towers rose at the corners of the walls, and the only small windows from which to see anyone who might approach the castle. The castles were often surrounded by a deep, wide trench or moat full of water. Over the moat, at the one entrance to the castle, was a bridge that could be drawn up to prevent unwelcome visitors from entering. The doorway to the castle was further protected by a grating of heavy planks, the portcullis, that could be dropped down quickly to close the entrance.

Carisbrooke Castle gatehouse

Within the castle walls was a great courtyard, at the farther end of which was the palace of the lord of the castle. Along one side of the walls was a great hall where the armed followers of

View of the Castle of Zafra, Campillo de Dueñas, Guadalajara, Spain. The castle was built in the late 12th or early 13th century on a sandstone outcrop and stands on the site of a former Visigothic and Moorish fortification that fell into Christian hands in 1129. It had considerable strategic importance as a virtually impregnable defensive work on the border between Christian and Muslim-ruled territory. The castle was never conquered and was successfully defended against the King of Castile in the 13th century. The successful completion of the Reconquista at the end of the 15th century ended its military significance.

the lord gathered in readiness to serve him, and across the court from the great hall were their barracks or sleeping quarters. Other buildings inside the walls were usually for storing supplies and arms. Also, there was usually a chapel, for these lords were Christian.

Around the castle lay the tracts of land owned by the lord of the manor (or *vil*), and the humble peasants who tilled the soil were his "villains." A portion of the estate was reserved by the lord for his own use; the rest was divided into long strips among the peasants. The peasants did not own these plots, but they could not be deprived of them as long as they worked for the lord and paid him certain dues. They had to plow and work his land and harvest his crops, and in addition, each serf might be asked to pay his lord, every year, one bushel of wheat, 18 sheaves of oats, three hens, one cock, and five eggs at Easter. The peasants' wives and daughters worked in the manor house (palace): spinning, weaving, sewing, baking, and brewing for the whole community. There was no opportunity for a peasant to better his condition. Generation after generation carried on a weary routine. The peasant's own hut was of one room with a single window and no chimney. The manor house was independent of the rest of the world. Little or no

Green grounds, Castell Beaumaris

money was necessary. As the peasants did all the work, the lord was free to busy himself fighting with other landowners in the same position as he was.

The peasants were not the lord's only "retainers" or followers. If he had a large estate with land to spare, he would offer it to another person on condition that the receiver would swear to be true to the giver and lend him aid against his enemies. Thus the vassal, upon receiving his fief, would kneel before the lord, place his hands between the hands of the lord and declare himself the lord's man for such and such fief. Thereupon, the lord gave his vassal the kiss of peace and raised him from his kneeling posture. Then the vassal would swear an oath of fidelity upon the Bible, promising to fulfill all his duties toward his lord. This ceremony, called "rendering homage," was the first duty of a vassal. Other duties included the giving of military aid, attending the court when summoned to give advice, and attending the lord on solemn occasions. Sometimes a vassal had to contribute money to his lord to help in payments of a dowry or a ransom. The vassal always had to be ready to entertain his lord should he visit the vassal's castle.

A vassal, in turn, might have vassals of his own, subvassals. Or, owners of small estates, being defenseless, often gave their land to a neighboring great lord and received it back from him as a fief, for the lord's agreement was always to protect his vassals when necessary. The fiefs were hereditary, passing to sons who likewise rendered homage. Vassals, like peasants, did not own the land, yet could not be deprived of it. The vassals of the king thus became quite independent as rulers of their own fiefs, and subvassals. Not having done homage to the king himself, they often paid little attention to his commands.

This was the feudal system. Such were the kingdoms of Europe, feudal castles scattered over wide lands, almost impassable roads, if any, from one fief to another. Yet these lords did not live peacefully apart from the world. Rather the law of the feudal world was war, in all its forms, so much so that a *feud* came to mean a continual quarrel.

Discontented vassals broke their oaths of fidelity or transferred their allegiance to another lord for the sake of better advantages. Refusal to do homage was the greatest way to revolt. A vassal would thus make war on his lord. He would make war on his fellow vassals, even upon his own vassals. Everyone was bent on taking advantage of someone weaker. A son, anxious to enjoy part of his inheritance immediately, would make war on the father. Brothers fought brothers who might seek to deprive them of their rights. The lords might call a court in order to settle a dispute peacefully, but they had not enough power to enforce the decisions of the Court, so the vassals were left to fight out their quarrels among themselves, and that was their chief interest in life. Jousts and tourneys (play wars) were military exercises to fill out the tiresome periods between real wars. In these battle games, whole troops of hostile nobles took part.

The bad roads, the lack of money, no commerce—these were obstacles to maintaining order. Land had to be paid instead of money. Hence a king could not pay an army. New invasions kept the people terrorized too. Moslems in Italy, Slavs in eastern Germany, Hungarians (Asiatics) in Germany and northern Italy, and Norsemen in the western Frankish kingdom—no wonder strong castles were built. Even the towns were surrounded by walls.

The horrors of this constant warfare led the Church to try to check it. About the year 1000 it proclaimed what was known as "The Truce of God," certain times when all warfare must cease: Lent (the forty days preceding Easter), other holy days, as well as Thursday, Friday, Saturday, and Sunday of every week. Those besieging castles were not to stage any assaults, and people were allowed to go about their business peacefully—plowmen, pilgrims, merchants—without being disturbed by soldiers. If anyone failed to observe the truce, he was excommunicated, which meant that if he fell sick, no Christian should dare to visit him, he would receive no comfort from a priest on his deathbed, and his soul would be consigned to hell. Many of the disorderly lords found three days a week altogether too short a time for plaguing their neighbors, and they ignored the truce completely.

The feudal castles were not the only great estates of this time. The dukes and counts and margraves were not the only landowners. The Church also owned great estates and, instead of castles, monasteries or abbeys provided shelter and protection especially from the pagans. Like the castles, the monasteries were often surrounded by high walls or were located on isolated hills, even cliffs, but they were not fortified. Their seclusion was not for the sake of military advantage but for the sake of solitude and quiet. Life in a castle was one of constant alarm, preparation for war, and recuperation from war. Life in a monastery was safe and peaceful. Kings and nobles, for the good of their souls, readily gave the land to the churchmen, and their rude, unscrupulous warriors seldom bothered to attack the monks who were believed to enjoy God's special favor. Studious or thoughtful men who disliked soldiering, and for whom such a time was dangerous and uncertain, could enter a monastery and find refuge there among the monks, and so could many friendless, disgraced, or even lazy people.

The monastery, like the castle, was built Roman country-house style around a court. This court was called the *cloister*. On all four sides of the cloister was a covered walk. At the north side was the church, always facing west. Along the west side were the storerooms. The refectory (dining room) and sitting room were to the south, and the dormitory was on the east. It adjoined the church in which there were seven services a day, the first before daybreak. Outside the monastery and around it were the garden, the orchard, the mill, the fish pond, the hospital, the guest house, and the grain fields.

The word *monk* comes from *monachus*, meaning "to live alone." Why were these monks who lived together named as if they lived alone?

Before Christianity, the Romans and Greeks had come to enjoy life in the world, with little thought of any other world except the "land of the shades," a place neither pleasant nor unpleasant, to which all souls departed after death

Franciscan monks in the cloister of Santa Maria in Ara Coeli, Rome

and about which they did not worry too much. They worshipped their gods to secure success and happiness in this world, not in the next. Christianity brought with it a new concern about one's life after death. This concern was so intense that thousands of men gave up their ordinary occupations and devoted their entire attention to preparation for life after death. They not only gave up occupations and all pleasures, but they inflicted punishment upon themselves hoping to avoid punishment in the next world. These men also withdrew from the world because of the sin and evil which surrounded them. In solitary cells they prayed and suffered, giving up all intercourse with this world to seek out the divine world.

These religious men were monks. Hundreds of them wandered to the East, as far as Egypt and Palestine, living in huts and caves by themselves, sustained by offerings of food. St. Anthony of Egypt lived many years as a hermit on the edge of the desert and was known everywhere as a holy man. Hosts of others followed him, each one living in his own cell in solitude, meeting with others for services only on Saturdays and Sundays. One such, in Syria more than 100 years before Mohammed was born, was St. Simeon Stylites, who lived for 30 years on top of a pillar just wide enough to lie on, increasing the height of his perch from 6 to 60 feet during that time. He hauled materials and supplies up by means of a basket at the end of a rope. Gradually, however, monks began to live together under one roof, in what came to be known as monasteries.

In the year 526, St. Benedict laid down the "Rule" according to which the monks in western monasteries should live:

- » candidates had to serve a novitiate;
- » abbots were elected by the brothers;
- » times of prayer, meditation, and worship had to be observed
- » three vows had to be taken: to be obedient to the abbot, to live in poverty, and never to marry.

Otherwise, the monks lived natural and busy lives, cultivating their fields, providing hospitality to travelers, copying the scriptures and the Latin writers, and serving as missionaries to the barbarians.

The castles were the strongholds of the descendants of the barbarian invaders of the Roman Empire. The monasteries were the strongholds of the Christian Church that had risen as Rome was dying.

PRIESTLY POWER and KINGLY POWER

When the officers of the Empire deserted their posts, the bishops stayed to meet the barbarians. They continued to represent the old civilization and ideas of order. They kept the Latin language alive and maintained some little education so they could read services and correspond with each other. Although the missionary monks had converted the people to Christianity, there was yet to be a conflict between them and the church. This was foreshadowed when one of the Bishops of Rome said, "Two powers govern the world, the priestly and the kingly. The first is assuredly the superior, for the priest is responsible to God for the conduct of even the emperors." And in light of this it was natural for the clergy to think that, in case of disagreement, the Church and its officers, rather than the King, should have the final word.

In this feudal age when, as we have seen, the King was powerless, it was the Church that governed the people in keeping order, managing education and trial of lawsuits, legalizing wills and marriages, and caring for widows and orphans.

In 445 CE, Valentian III, the Emperor of the West, had decreed that the Bishop of Rome, the Successor of St. Peter, was the Head of the Church. All other bishops throughout the West were to obey him and be forced to by the Imperial governors. The bishop of Rome came to be called the Pope, from the Latin *pater* or *papa* for "father."

Rome now ceased to be the Rome of the Caesars and became the Rome of the Popes who, after the Empire fell, began to govern Rome as well as the Church, to defend it against invaders, to make alliances with other nations, and to crown the kings and emperors, thus creating the situation in which the rulers of the Kingly Power in the West were such by consent of the Priestly Power.

However, just the opposite gradually arose. The kingly power became superior to the priestly, through the fact that many a lord, for the good of his soul, donated great estates to the bishops and abbots and, as fief holders, the churchmen thus became the vassals of the lords. These church lands could not pass by inheritance because the churchmen did not marry, and so when a landholding churchman died, someone had to be chosen in his place. Thus the bishops and abbots came to be appointed by the feudal lord who owned the land and had to render him homage and receive from him not only the land but the right to be a religious leader. In this way rough soldiers assumed the position to bestow religious powers, sometimes even making themselves bishops.

Now any man who wanted the honor and comfort of being an abbot, with lands and servants and revenues, could bribe a landowner to choose him as a bishop. Such a bishop, who had paid much for his office, then expected to get it out of the priests whom he appointed. The priest, having paid off the bishop, would try to get his money back by charging too much for baptizing, marrying, and burying his parishioners. So worldly were the clergy becoming (but not the monks), that they even began to marry and have children, which meant that their lands would go to their children at their death and not to the Church.

Thus, gradually, the Church was dragged down by its property into the state of feudalism, which was the character of kingly power, and in danger of becoming inferior to it.

MANUSCRIPTS and CATHEDRALS

During the dark ages of the barbarian invasions, the Church was the home of learning and art. In the shelter of the monasteries, the patient monks copied books and decorated them with colors and pictures. The monks made many beautiful books, copying the scriptures and prayers so they would not be forgotten. In each monastery there was a *scriptorium*, or writing room, where the copyists worked on parchment, with goose-quill pens and inks made with pigments and glue or acid.

Scriptorium

Such a book was the Anglo-Irish *Lindisfarne Gospels*, decorated so delicately and elaborately that it was hard to believe that it was done with human eyes and hands. These manuscripts were thought to work miracles. When the Danes invaded and burned or stole whatever they could lay their hands on, the Irish monks fled with these precious books, only to have them wash overboard and sink into the sea. It was a terrible tragedy and the monks could hardly sleep for sorrow. But one dreamed that St. Cuthbert appeared and told them to search along the shore, which they did and found the gospels lying on the sand as beautiful as ever.

These books could not be read by the common people, for they were written in Latin. However, the pictures could be understood and were copied onto the walls of churches or into the stained glass windows or in sculptures that the people could see when they went to worship.

The abbey, or monastery, was not a little kingdom in itself, as was the feudal estate, but was part of a whole chain of abbeys in France, England, Italy, and even Spain. The monks could come and go from abbey to abbey, taking their art and learning with them. Art and learning spread or lived wherever there were abbeys.

Speyer Cathedral, Germany

Eventually, as times became more settled, trade began to flourish between one feudal fief and another. By the 13th century many centers of trade had sprung up as towns in which the people wanted their own churches as separate from the abbeys—a town church or cathedral. Everyone wanted to do his share in building it, as a way of serving God. Craftsmen of every kind applied their skills, and if a man could do nothing else, he could hitch himself to a cart and draw stone for the building. The nobles and kings and queens were not ashamed to do their share. Every stone was someone's contribution, and the carvings and stained glass windows and paintings pictured the kings and queens of the Hebrews and scenes from the life of Christ, as well as the daily life of the people who worked on the cathedral, the harvesters, the hunters, the scholars, the knights, the kings and queens, the saints, and the goblins and the angels. Any person looking upon these pictures could feel, "There I am. I belong to this holy place." Not only did the community share in the building of a cathedral but it entered it to worship.

A Greek temple was the dwelling place of the god. The people, working in their fields around it, looking toward it but not entering it, had the feeling, "There stands the Temple with the indwelling god and I am near." In Christian times, growing out of the Hebrew, people wanted to separate their worship from everyday affairs. The temple or church became separate from the land, and its walls separated the space

Carlisle Cathedral, east window, Carlisle, UK

within from outer life. The Christian says, "I must leave my work and enter the church to worship God."

The Greek temple was supported by walls. The weight of the cathedral, the Gothic Church, was placed on the pillars so molded as to be able to bear the weight. As the walls were no longer needed for support, stained glass windows could be placed in them to open the church to light. The Gothic Cathedral was, and still is, a temple of light in which the worshiper can rise through meditation to God!

Porto Cathedral, Portugal

Henry IV and Gregory VII

Gregory VII, who became Pope in the year 1073, explained that the papal and the kingly powers are both established by God as the greatest among the authorities of the world, just as the sun and the moon are the greatest heavenly bodies, the papal power being the sun! Said Gregory, "The Pope is the only person whose feet are kissed by all the Princes."

Gregory VII

At this same time, a young German boy, fifteen years old, as Henry IV, became Emperor of the Holy Roman Empire. His first years were under the guidance of counselors who practiced the feudal system by granting fiefs and selecting the bishops of these fiefs, so that these bishops became Henry's vassals. It was imperative that, if the Church was to have authority over its bishops, it must have the power of selecting them.

Henry IV of England

Pope Gregory forbade the "lay investiture" of bishops. When Henry's counselors rebelled, the Pope excommunicated them, but Henry continued to associate with these counselors. The Pope then threatened the Emperor not only with excommunication but with the permanent loss of all his royal honors. Henry then summoned a council at Worms (1076) of more than two-thirds of all the German bishops, who then proclaimed that Gregory had ceased to be their Pope. The Pope's reply was to call upon St. Peter with these words:

> Incline thine ear to us, O Peter, Chief of the Apostles. As thy representatives and by thy favor has the power been granted especially to me, by God, of binding and loosing in heaven and earth. On the strength of this, for the honor and glory of thy Church, in the name of Almighty Father, Son, and Holy Ghost, I withdraw from Henry, who has risen against thy Church with unheard of insolence, the rule over the whole kingdom of the Germans and over Italy. I absolve all Christians from the bonds of oath they have sworn, or may swear, to him; and I forbid anyone to serve him as king.

Thus was Henry excommunicated and deposed. The rebellious counselors invited the Pope to Augsburg to help them select another king, but Henry hastened to Italy first, where, barefoot and dressed in the coarse robes of a pilgrim and a penitent, he knelt for three days outside the Pope's closed door before being admitted and pardoned. This was not the end of Henry's troubles, for his enemies rose against him more than once. Even his son revolted.

Henry IV abdicated in 1104 and died in 1106. Henry V and the new Pope then came to an agreement: The bishops already chosen by the king, if worthy, might continue in office. The clergy need no longer do homage and lay their hands in the "blood-stained" hands of the nobles. The Church was to elect bishops and abbots in the presence of the King who, in a separate ceremony, would by touch of his scepter invest them with fiefs and powers to govern, and he could, if he wished, refuse lands to those selected by the Church.

The Popes had been elected by the cardinals, the Princes of the Church, without sanction of the Emperor, since 1059. A hundred years later, in 1152, the Lord of the castle Hohenstaufen in southern Germany was elected as Emperor by the German nobles without sanction of the Pope. In fact he announced to the Pope that he had been chosen as Emperor by God. He was Frederick I, called Barbarossa because of his red beard.

Now both the Kingly Power and the Priestly Power claimed to be established by God, and what was to develop much later had its beginning—the separation of Church and State.

The Culture of the Moors

In contrast to feudalism north of the Pyrenees, the Moorish Khalifs in Spain had built up a wondrous civilization. On the banks of the Guadalquiver River, five miles from Cordova, was the Khalif's palace named Medina-al-Zohra (Town of the Flower). It was built of Greek marble on a Roman foundation. There were 4300 columns of marble, marble pavements, and rooms with fountains in basins of porphyry (quartz crystals). In the Khalif's Hall the fountain was made of jasper (yellow quartz), and the water spouted from the bill of a golden swan, beneath a canopy in the center of which was a great pearl, a gift from the Emperor of Constantinople. The woodwork was of cedar. In the midst of a garden where beautiful shrubs and flowers were arranged to delight all beholders, there was a fountain of quicksilver.

Music was greatly cultivated by the Moors. Not only did they sing, but they wrote books about the elements of music and wrote down musical notation. One book still remains containing 150 airs.

Everyone was a poet! The extraordinary richness of their language was such that the dictionary filled sixty volumes. Princes challenged each other in poetry contests. Storytellers were held in high honor.

History, grammar, rhetoric, and philosophy were written about to an extent never dreamed of by Mohammed. Mathematics was studied in earnest. *Gebr*, the Arabic term for arithmetic, is the source of our "algebra." Wise men of Cordova applied their knowledge of math to astronomy. They named the individual stars. The geography of Spain was studied as well as the scenery, inhabitants, productions, and natural history of other countries. Agriculture was a study, and books were written on irrigation, crops, cattle, grafting, and gardening. The motto of the Arab landowner was, "He who planteth and soweth, and maketh the earth bring forth fruit for man and beast, hath done alms that shall be reckoned to him in heaven." Some of the plant names we know come from the Spanish Arabs, for example:

- » *albaric aque* → apricot
- » *alco chofa* → artichoke
- » *al godon* → cotton

Cordova was the seat of the great literary society where the descendants of Arab sheiks opened their gorgeous palaces in the evenings to poets and philosophers and men of science who debated and recited as in the days of Pericles. Travelers and adventurers told of their discoveries.

The Khalif's library contained books made by scribes whom he had sent to Egypt, Syria, Persia, and Greece. The books were written on paper, for the Arabs had learned how to make paper from the Chinese. To this library all learned men could come to study and to lecture. Here came many a Christian scholar, too, and made himself acquainted with the Arabic translations of the literature and science of pre-Roman times.

This Moorish civilization, which made Spain into a center of learning, flourished for hundreds of years and was the gateway through which the ancient cultures finally made their entrance into the West. So it was that, although the Moors themselves could not penetrate into France and other countries of Europe, their culture had a great effect on the development of Western culture.

In the meantime, to the East, in the realms of the Eastern Khalif, new waves of barbarians began to wash down over the land from Asia. William of Normandy had become King of England in the year 1066. In 1076, tribes known as the Turks came out of Central Asia and took possession of Jerusalem, having conquered Constantinople in 1071. The Turks were followers of Mohammed. Fierce and fanatical, they proclaimed Mohammed as the messenger of God and did not tolerate the Christians but made slaves of them and destroyed their churches.

Excerpts from the History of England

55 BC - 1453 CE

In contrast to the desert lands of the Arabs, someone offered this description of the British Isles:

> *A wide, silver sea,*
> *an unbroken dome of sky*
> *across which the clouds roll*
> *in endless columns,*
> *shedding a silver light earthward*
> *from their dark flanks,*
> *and dark, low-lying stretches of land*
> *swimming in the ocean;*
> *where the weather is constantly changing*
> *from sunlight on cloud and water*
> *to mist and rain, to sunlight again.*

UTHYR
(meaning *Wonderful*)

The Dark Ages were the centuries that followed the downfall of Rome in the West. They were dark because the events of history that followed this downfall were like a dark curtain drawn over all that had been civilized in the Western world.

In Britain, when the Romans withdrew, all that had been built up fell into disuse. As in Europe, roads fell into disrepair, governments fell apart, trade stopped, people were in fear of their neighbors, and the tribal wars began, with the invasions of the Saxons, Angles, and Jutes. There was bloodshed. There were turmoil, destruction, restlessness, fear, and revenge.

Yet while this darkness of spirit was at its blackest, there was also shining a light which never flickered out, with a power to shine even in the stormiest times and places. It was not a physical light but the Light in the hearts of certain men who carried the blessing and peace of Christ to people who lived in the most remote parts of Britain and Ireland. These men were the Celtic monks whose lives were wonderful and brave. Their message brought hope of a new kind of life to despairing people. "Thou shalt love the Lord, thy God, with all thy heart, with all thy soul, with all thy mind, and with all thy strength, and thy neighbor as thyself."

In pre-Christian times the Celtic people followed the religion of the Druids who worshipped the star-filled cosmos of which the sun is the heart. The Druids taught that life on earth would be right and harmonious in so far as it reflected the life of the heavens. They looked up to the stars as the home of the gods. As seers they perceived that the Lord of Light, whose dwelling was in the sun, left his abode to enter the earth and an earthly body. When this happened, the sun ceased to be the true temple of the Light but continued to shine in the image of the Lord of Light, giving to the world through the changes of time its grace of light, life, and warmth. And so it came to pass that the followers of the Druids heard and understood that He, who was God of the sun, had come to be King of the elements that move over the earth.

In the Latin Chronicles, written by Geoffrey of Monmouth before the middle of the 12th century, the writer traces the Celtic people who were living in England before Roman times back to Brutus, a great-grandson of Aeneas. Brutus landed on these misty shores when the island was called Albion. According to this legend, Brutus found the island inhabited by a race of giants who were evidently neither too bold nor too brave, for Brutus and his companions forced them to flee into mountain caves and then settled themselves on the land, tilling the ground and building houses. Brutus gave the land his own name, Britain, and the people were named Britons.

These were the Britons whom Julius Caesar subdued in 55 BC, but they were not to be truly conquered by Rome for another hundred years. These Britons, or Celts, had been there for a long time and remained to be civilized under Roman rule for 400 years, until Alaric the Goth attacked Rome in 408 CE. When the Roman legions left Britain to go to the defense of their native land, then from the north, the still barbarous Picts and Scots invaded the lands of the Celts who had no means of defending themselves now that the Roman armies were gone. However, the Celts knew of warrior-men across the channel in Angle-land, Saxe-land, and Jute-land. Indeed, many of these "Englisc" folk had become ruthless pirates on the sea and skimmed the British shores in their ships. So the Celts sent for them to come to their aid.

In the year 449 CE, led by two brothers from Jute-land, Hengist and Horsa, the pirates answered the call for help, landed in Britain, and drove off the Scots and Picts. Liking the country well, they decided to conquer the Celts, too, and make the country their own.

ARTHUR

The skies are painted with unnumbered sparks;
they all are fire and every one doth shine;
but there's but one in all doth hold his place.
— William Shakespeare

Then rose a Celtic hero to defend the land. His stronghold lay in Cornwall, in Tintagel Castle by the Cornish Sea. He was said to be a descendant of Brutus, the descendant of Aeneas. Throughout his reign as King, this hero, Arthur, fought the pagans (Saxons), for Arthur was a Christian king.

When we look at the starry sky, we have a sensation of a great multitude of stars. If we would watch them night after night, we would see that certain ones remain together, while others move through the groups that remain together; but they all move through the night sky in a grand procession from east to west, rising and setting in the same direction that the sun rises and sets.

Upon closer observation, we would notice that in the northern sky certain groups of stars do not rise up and then set below the horizon, but they do not stand still. They circle around the sky like the parts of a great wheel that is ever turning around its axle, marked by a star that does not change its position but acts like the hub of the wheel.

This star, the center of the wheel, was called the "Veralder Nagli," the World Spike, by the Norsemen who guided their ships in relation to it. To their belief, this World Spike held creation together and was the axis of both heaven and earth, a spar so mighty that the earth and all the stars of heaven revolved around it. They imagined that the end of the spike was firmly fastened to the outer rim of the universe by means of a jeweled nailhead, which was that star around which all the others revolved.

A story tells that a boy of Celtic lineage fell asleep on the seashore. A spirit guided him far to the north, from whence were to come a people who were to be his enemies when he grew to manhood. However, he found himself not in a northern land but in a northern sky. And there, seated at a great circular table shining with starlight, he was surrounded by noble beings who spoke to him and gave him wise counsel. They told him his name would be Uthyr, meaning Wonderful, and that he should pattern his life and the rule of his kingdom on that of the Kingdom of Heaven.

When this boy became a king on earth, he was named Arthur, and he gathered around him a circle of knights in a round table modeled after that round table he had seen in the skies. These knights were the wisest and bravest men he could find in the land.

If you can imagine a mingling of the spirit of feudal times and the love of battle with the gentleness and selflessness of the Celtic saints, you would be able to understand what a true knight was. No one was born a knight. A man could be born as prince or duke, but he had to win knighthood, either through training as a page and squire or as a reward for gallant deeds.

The chevalier, who in pagan times was so-called because he fought on horseback and was a noble, became something more than just a warrior, after Christianity was spread among the people. He was christened as well as knighted. As a knight he followed a rule of service, of loyalty, of fearlessness in the cause of the right, of truthfulness in word and deed, of courtesy and generosity, and of consideration for those in distress and need. The knight who acted against this rule was a false knight, a "recreant" knight, and all true knights were against him.

The training for knighthood began when a boy became a page, at about 7 years of age. At 15 or 16, the page was ready to become a squire who accompanied his lord to tournament and war, took care of his armor, armed him, fought by his side ready to protect him, and carried him to safety should he be wounded.

Many a squire never became a knight, for the life of a knight was filled with discomforts, and those who had no gaiety, no sense for adventure, but who preferred the security of their manors, settled down to being lords of the land. Those who loved "adventures," as knightly deeds were called, and who could meet discomfort and distress with gaiety of spirit—they sought knighthood with all their heart and soul.

What were these adventures?
- » To clear forests of outlaws
- » To subdue and fight the robber barons
- » To help and deliver damsels in distress
- » To try skill in jousts and tournaments against other knights.

True knights loved to wander in search of adventures and hence were called "knights-errant." Those who were the greatest were described as courteous, true, kind, goodly, meek, and stern; and with all these great and good qualities they must needs be ready to fight to the last breath.

In the great stories of King Arthur and his Knights of the Round Table, we hear of adventures that tested not only the strength and skills of battle, but also the spirit of knighthood. Those who were at first pure and noble in their deeds were in time overcome by what was evil in themselves, and Arthur died in his last great battle forsaken by all but one, Sir Belvedere.

When Arthur died, it was believed that his soul traveled back to those northern skies, those northern stars, and that from there he would return again to rule over England. Ursa Major, the Great Bear or the Big Dipper, which circles the Pole Star, is also known as Arthur's Chariot, and a "Round Table" is drawn by its tail as it swings around Polaris.

ALFRED THE GREAT
Ruled 871–901 CE

Alfred was the son of Aethewulf, the King of the West Saxons, and became King of Wessex when he was twenty-two years old. He had to devote the first seven years of his rule to warfare against the Danes who were seeking to invade Wessex. In 878 he defeated them and made peace with a Danish king, Guthrum, who became a Christian and was allowed to rule in Danelaw, a region northeast of Wessex. The peace lasted about fifty years.

Alfred had visited Rome three times before he was ten years old. There he had seen the Pope and a civilization far different from that in Wessex. In spite of the seven years of warfare, he sought peace and justice for his subjects. He is called "the father of the British navy" because he saw to it that his ship builders made boats that could carry more men than the Danish ships. He loved Saxon poetry and the Christian prayer book, which he carried with him all his life, even in battle.

Alfred is the only English king called "the Great." The reasons for this have been noted by many historians. As a ruler he collected the laws in use throughout his kingdom and had them written down, then chose the ones that seemed best. He added some of his own making and consulted with the Witan (council) for their approval. He divided his kingdom into districts where the people had a say in their local affairs, and this was reported to the King by the officers whom he appointed to represent him in each district. Alfred valued learning and scholarship and the things of the spirit. He translated, and had others translate, many books from Latin into Saxon so that his people would not remain ignorant. He encouraged the writing of a history of Britain, "The Anglo-Saxon Chronicle," which was continued for 150 years after his death. He devoted regular hours by day and by night to worship and prayer. One historian described him in these words: "He was especially and wonderfully kind toward all men, and merry. And to the searching out of all things not known did he apply himself with all his heart."

Such a man gave wisdom to his people. His wise sayings, treasured by them, include proverbs like these:
» Eyes are of no use to the blindly minded.
» Keep your new friend and your wine until they are old.
» The much-talker strips his mind of its real merit.
» Power is never good unless he be good that hath it.

Here is a thought, a sort of prayer, that guided his rule: "Ah! Wise One, thou knowest that greed and the possession of this earthly power never were pleasing to me, nor did I ever desire this earthly kingdom, save that I desired tools and materials to do the work that it was commanded me to do. A king's raw material and instruments of rule are a well-peopled land—and men of prayer, men of war, men of work." It was from out of this thoughtful wisdom that he encouraged the churchmen, the soldiers, and the men who cultivated the land.

EDWARD THE CONFESSOR
Ruled 1042–1066

After Alfred's death, England came under the rule of Danish kings, the greatest of whom was King Canute, a Christian king and beloved of his subjects. He married the widowed mother of a young Saxon whose name was Edward and who became King after Canute's death. Edward's mother was a Norman and Edward was brought up as a Norman. When he came to England as its King, he brought with him a following of Normans, mainly monks and churchmen. Edward himself was more like a monk than a king, and his holiness of life won him the name "Confessor." He was sanctified in the 12th century and is often spoken of as "Saint Edward."

As King of England, Edward put the burden of government on the district rulers, the earls, the most powerful of whom was the Saxon, Earl Godwin. King Edward enforced the laws of Alfred the Great. After Edward's death he was given the title "Arthur" because he had worked for the best traditions of England. William Caxton, the printer of Sir Thomas Malory's *Morte d'Arthur*, wrote in the preface of this book, "In the Abbey of Westminster, at Edward's shrine, remaineth the print of his seal in red wax closed in beryl in which it is written, 'Patricius Arthurus, Britannie, Gallie, Germanie, Dacie, Imperator.'"

After Saint Edward's death and soon to be under Norman rule, the people often longed for the laws and customs of the good King Edward. Edward left no heir. The Saxon, Harold, son of Earl Godwin, was elected King by the Earls.

THE NORMANS

For years the Western Frankish lands were subject to raids by the Vikings, or Norsemen, who were in search of booty. In the year 911 Hrolf (Rollo), one of the Norse chieftains, was granted a fief along the coast of the channel between France and Britain. Rollo became Duke of the Normans, whose countryside became Normandy. In time the Norman dukes became so powerful that they could not easily be controlled by the King of France.

WILLIAM OF NORMANDY
King William I of England
Ruled 1066–1087

When Harold Godwin was elected King of England, the powerful Duke William of Normandy claimed that King Edward had promised him the English throne. As Harold ignored his claim, William recruited thousands of fighting men and began to build a fleet of ships in which to cross the English Channel, to land and camp on the plain of Hastings, south of London, and to conquer Britain

In October 1066, Harold was called to northern England to repel an invasion by a fresh wave of Norsemen who had landed and were devastating coastal towns. He put them to flight, but while at the victory banquet, he received word that William of Normandy had crossed the channel, landing with his soldiers on the southern coast, and was camped on the plain of Hastings. It was autumn and a large part of Harold's men had gone home to harvest their crops. So he had to hurry south with an insufficient army to join battle with the Normans, a battle that was to end the Anglo-Saxon rule of Britain. The Normans, with their longbows and horsemen, overcame the Saxons, mostly on foot, whose swords and axes called for close-range fighting. Harold was killed by a Norman arrow that pierced his eyes.

William "the Conqueror" now became King of England and was crowned in Westminster Abbey on Christmas Day, 1066. The estates of those who had fought against him were given to the Normans who had fought with him. Then he made every landowner his vassal so that no other overlord could call upon any vassal to fight against him as king, and no noble could summon his vassal to war against another noble without the King's permission. In this way he overcame the weaknesses of the feudal system.

When he had thus established his authority, King William surveyed what he had conquered and listed all the estates that had become his property so that he might collect taxes from each. This list was published as "The Domesday Book."

He established London as his capital city. There he built offices in which the money matters of his new kingdom could be accounted for: the tax collections and the expenditures in maintaining an army of soldiers who were to see that the laws were obeyed and to protect the people of the realm from robbers and bandits. William kept many of the old Saxon laws, added new ones based on Roman law, and allowed the people to carry on local government as before. He also allowed the Church to govern itself.

The King, however, set aside the forests as hunting grounds for himself and his Norman friends, and Norman French became the official court language. The English language expanded to include words from French, Latin, Danish, and Anglo-Saxon. Norman castles and churches sprang up throughout England.

King William died in 1087 after an injury suffered when he fell off his horse. He was only 52 years old. This was nine years before the First Crusade in 1096. After William's death, his heirs had a difficult time keeping order in England and at the same time ruling their lands in Normandy where they had to spend a great part of their time.

Now many Normans emigrated and settled in England. Within 100 years after William's death, the whole body of nobility, bishops, abbots, dukes and so on, were practically all Normans. By the year 1200 even the lower classes of merchants, tradesmen, and craftsmen had become mixed with the Norman people.

THE PLANTAGENETS

France and England were not yet separate nations. They were more like feudal estates with Frenchmen ruling in England as English kings who in turn claimed large territories in France. The youngest son of William I (of Normandy) ruled England as Henry I from 1100–1135. His daughter, Mathilda, married Geoffrey Plantagenet, the Count of Anjou, and their son became Henry II, King of England from 1154–1189. The family name was now Plantagenet, but the royal line founded in England by Henry Plantagenet is called the Angevin (of Anjou) line.

Henry II strengthened the power of the English kingship in England by weakening the powers of the nobles, by introducing the jury system, and by establishing the practice of a common law throughout England. At the same time, he ruled wide lands in France: Normandy, which he had inherited from his father, and Aquitaine, which was inherited by his wife, Eleanor. Henry's possessions in France were greater than his kingdom in England. He even controlled more land in France than did the French King (Louis VII) himself; yet, as King of England, he was vassal to the French King.

Thomas à Becket, the Archbishop of Canterbury, was a close friend of Henry II. They quarreled over the question as to whether the kingly power or the Church's power was the greater. When the Archbishop refused to admit that the king had more authority than the Church, the king's complaints were overheard by men loyal to the king, and they attacked and murdered Thomas à Becket in Canterbury Cathedral.

The death of Thomas à Becket shocked the Christian world, and the King did public penance, begging the pardon of Becket at his tomb in Canterbury (1174). Already the tomb had become a place of pilgrimages and was immortalized in Chaucer's *Canterbury Tales*. Thomas à Becket was canonized as a saint in 1173.

Thomas à Becket

Richard the Lion Heart

Henry II had three sons and divided his French lands among them: Geoffrey, who died in 1186; John; and Richard, who was the oldest and who succeeded him as King of England. Richard, the Lion-hearted, a most famous knight in battles, was a poor king. He sought adventure in the Third Crusade.

A few years before Henry II died, the son of Louis VII had come to the French throne. He was Philip Augustus, and King Richard sought him out as his companion in the Crusade. When they quarreled, Philip abandoned Richard and returned to France, there to make trouble for Richard in his French possessions. Philip spent his life trying to gain power over the Plantagenets.

In the meantime, with Richard away on a crusade, John made himself King. Richard never actually ruled England, for when he returned from the Crusade, he found England at war with Philip, and in the midst of this, he died.

Now was the time when the English first began to consider themselves as separate from France. King John refused to do homage to Philip Augustus, and so Philip seized the lands in France that belonged to the Plantagenets. When John tried to gather an army of English nobles to reconquer his French lands, the nobles refused on the ground that their feudal vows did not bind them to fight outside their own country. They regarded John as a tyrant and forced him to sign a promise, the Magna Carta, which included two guarantees of justice and freedom which are a part of our own law today, that:

» no taxes can be levied without the consent of the King's Council (today, our Congress);
» and no free man can be punished for any crime without a fair trial by a court of his peers.

After King John signed the Magna Carta, he tried to break his promise, but neither he nor any later king could get rid of the document. When John's son, Henry III, disregarded the charter, he was imprisoned, and Simon de Montfort, Earl of Leicester, started the first parliament, or assembly, to curb the kingly powers in favor of the power of the people.

In the following years, the descendants of the Plantagenets—Edward I, Edward II, and Edward III—carried the course of history forward to the point, in 1346, when Edward III led an army into France to begin what became The Hundred Years' War between France and England, a period lasting until 1453.

The Crusades

1096 - 1291

The Start of the Crusades

Looking down on the lands of Europe and Asia, around the Mediterranean Sea, we now see:

- » in Asia, a new barbarian empire,
- » in Spain, intellectual culture, wealth, and comfort,
- » in Europe, feudalism, war, struggles for power between the Church and landowners, with the Church trying hard to win absolute power.

We now must look into the hearts of the people who were not in a position to wage war and to win power, in this instance the hearts of the Christian people, the poor, the meek, the humble. Whether they were Western or Eastern Christians, in their hearts they turned against the powerful and tyrannical rulers of the Churches and, in their discontent, longed to find Christ himself in the world.

They hoped to find him in the Holy Land where he had lived. In their devotion to him, they sought him out on the soil where he had walked. Those who could, over many years, left their homes, their fields, their lords and journeyed as pilgrims to the Holy Land where the sight of the places where Christ had been made them feel purer and nearer to Heaven.

In the Holy Land they would follow him from the cave where he was born to the mount where he had preached, to Golgotha where he had died, and to his tomb, or sepulcher, in Jerusalem, over which stood a church in which the Cross of Christ was reverenced. Before the Turks captured the city of the Holy Sepulcher and the Holy Land (1071), the Christian pilgrims were permitted access to their shrines by the Khalif of the East.

In spite of two monks, Augustine and Jerome, who said, "Righteousness was not to be sought in the East nor mercy in the West, and voyages were useless to carry us to him who is everywhere present," more and more thousands of pilgrims from almost every country of Europe took their way to Palestine.

In the year 1000, the end of the first millennium CE, all Christians looked to the second coming of Christ and the day of judgment when the dead would rise from their graves and ascend to Heaven, and the weary, sin-laden world would come to an end. But no such thing happened. The sun continued to rise and set as before, the sinful world became more sinful, and the flood of pilgrims increased. Men of all classes and ranks left their homes to offer up their prayers at the tomb of Christ, even bishops and princes. Those who died on the way because of the hardships they suffered were considered blessed beyond all others, became as Holy as the Innocents who had been killed by King Herod.

When, in 1076, the East came under the power of the Turks, a dreadful change took place. Along all the pathways that made up the Road of God to Jerusalem, the pilgrims were attacked by Turkish warriors and robbed and beaten. The patriarch (high priest) in Jerusalem was kidnapped, dragged by his hair along the pavement, thrown into a dungeon, and there held for a high ransom. So great were the calamities to the Christians in the East, that the West was roused to a high pitch of indignation and anger. The Pope, Urban II, was angry too, but he had his own troubles in the West. Another man was trying to depose him and become Pope in his place. Urban was also having troubles with clergy who had married and refused to abandon their wives. He had to excommunicate the "King of France," a feudal lord. All these affairs were more important to him than the people's demand that help be sent to the Holy Land. He put this off.

Yet it became necessary for him to meet with the bishops of his realm, and he crossed the Alps into France, proceeding to Clermont. There he found thousands of people crowded into the town and camped in tents around it; and from their midst there came forward a man, with bare head and bare feet, riding on an ass and carrying a huge crucifix. He was dwarfish in stature, thin and emaciated, and in his eyes burned a fiery earnestness that had a powerful effect upon the throngs who surrounded him.

This was a man named Peter. He was a Frenchman who had been a soldier of one of the counts of Boulogne but who had laid aside his sword, forsaken his wife, and become a hermit. In history he is remembered as Peter the Hermit. Like others, he had had the irresistible longing to visit the Holy Land and to pray at the tomb of Christ. He had found it in the hands of the Turkish "infidels." He had found the patriarch enslaved and Christian men being murdered and women being wronged. He had made a vow that, with the help of God, such wrongs would cease. Now he had returned to the West to gather an army to march against the infidels. Wherever he went, he stirred up the people to want to deliver the Holy Land from the Turks. As he spoke of the horrors he had seen,

Peter the Hermit and Alexius Comnenus

his voice was choked with sobs and groans, and all who heard him wept and cried out. He promised that all personal sins would be wiped out and forgiven for those who would take part in redeeming the Holy Land.

Now he spoke before Pope Urban, pleading with him to call together the Christian armies. Now the Pope could no longer put off concerning himself with what he should do in the East. The Council of Bishops and Abbots was called upon to consider what best be done. Then Urban spoke to the crowds awaiting his word, and called upon Christian men to lay aside their private quarrels and discords and unite for the redemption of the Holy Sepulcher. As he ended, there was an outcry among the thousands, "It is the will of God! It is the will of God!"

Then said the Pope, "Let this be your war cry when you unsheathe your swords against the enemy. You are soldiers of the Cross: wear, then on your breasts or shoulders the blood-red sign of Him who died for the salvation of your souls. Wear it as a token that His help will never fail you; wear it as a pledge, a vow, which can never be recalled."

In a short time some 60,000 men and women insisted that Peter the Hermit should lead them at once to the Holy City. Peter, aided by a poor knight, Walter the Penniless, undertook to do so.

"Deus Vult"

Deus Vult! It is the will of God! The outcry of the people became the war cry.

When the Eastern Emperor Alexius sent to Pope Urban II for help against the Turks, Urban thought of several things:

- » If the Kings of Europe would lead their knights against the infidels, that might put a stop to their quarrels.
- » If the Western Christians recovered the Holy Land, it might lead to a reunification of the Eastern and Western Churches.
- » Such a unification would make the Church more powerful than the unruly feudal lords and their followers.

In the light of such thoughts, he called upon the kings and their vassals to lead armies to the East to fight for the recovery of the Holy Land. "Go forward bravely," he said, "and justify your knighthood in warring as soldiers of the Lord! Set out on this journey and you will be forgiven your sins and be sure of the glory of the Kingdom of Heaven."

He also promised the crusaders cancellation of their debts, freedom to serfs and prisoners, and new lands. His exhortation to all people was, "He that taketh not his cross and followeth after me is not worthy of me."

"Taking the Cross" was the name of the vow of the crusader, whatever his rank. He wore the sign of the Cross on his breast on the way to Jerusalem and on his back when he returned.

So, for the next two hundred years, the crusades continued, at intervals of time. The people who followed great leaders were varied. There were the religious and devout, the romantic and adventurous, the discontented nobles, merchants interested in trade, vagabonds wishing no responsibility at home, criminals and robbers. Some went alone, some in small groups, and thousands in vast hordes. They were attacked by the peoples whose countries they went through, or they suffered starvation and died, or fell by the way because of disease, or were captured and sold as slaves.

Descriptions from chronicles of that time provide us with vivid details:

"Most of the first crusaders marched afoot, with some carts and pack animals, and little food could be transported. The meat supply went on the hoof. There were no maps. Road were merely trails from village to village. Main highways were the remnants of Roman roads. Having no money, the travelers had to trade their gear and valuables for supplies."

"A barren land, both pathless and mountainous. It was winter and we saw neither birds nor beasts for thrice seven days. We wandered through low-hanging clouds so dense that we were able to feel them often to push them away from us as we moved."

"Plodding through immense and indescribable forests, we had to fight for grain, oil, and cattle; had to build rafts at the rivers and sometimes to manage without rafts.

"Then we came to the swift river 'Demon' which is rightly named. For we had to watch many of our people, wading across step by step, swept down by the current. If the knights had not brought their great battle chargers to aid those on foot, many more would have perished."

"Hunger troubled us constantly and we had almost nothing to eat except thorns that we pulled off and rubbed between our hands. The greater part of our horses died so that many riders became foot soldiers. Some rode oxen; and goats, sheep, and dogs served to carry our baggage."

"Whoever heard so many languages in a single army? We were Franks, Flemings, Gauls, Bavarians, Lombards, Normans, Angles, Scots, Italians, Bretons, Greeks. If a Breton spoke to me, I did not know how to answer."

(In the Taurus Mountains) "We entered a defile of the devil, so lofty and steep that we hardly dared to press ahead along the path. Horses fell bodily, and one pack animal dragged another with it. The knights beat themselves with their hands for grief in this place. And so we passed through the accursed mountain and came to a city called Marash. The inhabitants, Christian Armenians, came out joyfully to meet us and there we all had plenty."

The Crusades
(1096–1291 CE)

In 1096, when Peter the Hermit and Walter the Penniless set out with five companies, they were ill-equipped. Led by emotion rather than reason, it was a disorderly host of undisciplined men who had enthusiasm but little else. Through hunger, fatigue, illness, and attacks by Turks and Hungarians, all perished before reaching Jerusalem.

By the end of the year, four knights leading their own companies of men reached Constantinople. Of these, Godfrey de Bouillon was the leader. A brave and chivalrous knight, a stern and merciless warrior, he desired only to fight for his faith and to free the Holy Land. He sought nothing for himself. He was the first and last to win Jerusalem by force of arms. No later Crusade succeeded in this beyond making temporary peace treaties with the Saracens.

Godfrey led what is called the First Crusade. From France he went by land down the Danube Valley, then southeast to Constantinople, where he took the oath of fealty to the Emperor Alexius. He was then permitted to go into Asia Minor. He besieged and conquered Nicaea and Antioch (an eight-month siege). Those who were with him quarreled among themselves, each seeking territory for himself. His brother, Baldwin, captured Edessa and made himself Prince thereof. Bohemond, the Norman leader, and Raymond, the Count of Toulouse, had a

Godfrey of Bouillon
and leaders of the first crusade

bitter quarrel as to who should have Antioch. Bohemond won the claim and Raymond went on to conquer Tripoli as his territory. These three set up their own feudal estates, built castles, and ruled as if they were at home.

In 1099, three years after leaving France, Godfrey led his forces of 20,000 against Jerusalem and besieged it from June 6th to July 15th. The warriors, upon entering the city, became beasts, massacring the entire population without pity. "Such a slaughter of pagan folk had never been seen or heard of; none knew their number save God alone. After slaughtering Saracens all day long nearby, at nightfall the crusaders, sobbing for joy, went to kneel at the Holy Sepulcher, the Tomb of the Prince of Peace."

Godfrey, who had led them to victory and whose part in the slaughter is not mentioned, but who would not have stopped it if he could, was chosen King of Jerusalem. He refused to be crowned a king, saying he would not wear a crown of gold in the place where his Lord had worn a crown of thorns. He took the title "Defender of the Holy Sepulcher" and as such remained in Jerusalem for one year. When he died, his brother, Baldwin, took his place and did not hesitate to call himself "King of Jerusalem." He was succeeded by many other kings of Jerusalem for the next 200 years. Many of them inherited the title while ruling their domains in Europe.

The Second Crusade was called for by Bernard of Clairvaux, a monk and a Knight Templar, who never went to the Holy Land himself but incited others to do so. Jerusalem had been in the hands of the Christian kings for eighty odd years, and feudal estates had been established by Franks in the Holy Land by then, but the Moslems were by no means defeated. In 1146 CE the Turks attacked and captured Edessa, the capital of the estate that Count Baldwin had first taken for himself. Now, led by Kings Louis VII of France and Conrad III of Germany, two new armies met in Acre on the eastern Mediterranean coast and, in consultation with King Baldwin III of Jerusalem and other leaders, they decided to attack Damascus, a Turkish stronghold. They laid siege to it, but when they heard that a strong Turkish force was on its way to bring relief to the city, they withdrew. This was the end of the Second Crusade.

The Third Crusade took shape about forty years later, in 1187 CE. There appeared a new Moslem leader, Saladin, the Sultan of Egypt and Syria, whose aim was to reunite the Moslems and their lands under his rule. To gain time to rally the Moslem nations and to recapture Palestine, he made a truce with Baldwin. A French noble, Reynald, Lord of Outer Jordan, who had come to find his fortune in the East, broke the truce by attacking a Moslem caravan and robbing it of

Saladin

everything it carried. Saladin then took revenge. He led an army into Palestine, won victory after victory over the Christian fortress-cities, and surrounded Jerusalem. The inhabitants of the city had no hope and surrendered to him on October 2, 1187. "The Eastern Empire of the Franks has crashed into ruin."

The story of the Third Crusade is the story of Richard Coeur de Lion, King of England, who tried to recapture Jerusalem. It was a hundred years after the first crusade, during the years 1190–1192. This crusade was also called "the Kings' Crusade" because the King of England was joined by Philip Augustus, the King of France, and Frederick Barbarossa, the King of Germany.

Richard the Lion Heart on His Way to Jerusalem

In contrast to Godfrey de Bouillon's long and painful march to the Holy Land from France, we see Richard sailing from Marseilles in a long, red galley with a dragon's head on the prow and a fine cloth canopy hung over the afterdeck. It was a model of the Viking ships of Richard's Norman ancestors, with a row of shields painted over the oars. Thus, in gay array, he led his fleet to the Holy Land. His stops along the way were very different from the dangers that had beset Godfrey's crusaders a century before. Wherever he stopped, the knights and men-at-arms manned the rails of his ship with uplifted spears, while pennons flew from the masthead. Trumpets sounded as the royal galley was beached. Steps were placed for the King to descend over the prow. Horses and attendants were landed from another craft and the King's charger led forth for him to mount.

The crusaders lived on the decks of the ships that were in the fleet. Cages of poultry and open fires for cooking shared the space where they slept, ate, and walked. In the sand ballast of the hold was wine, thus kept cool. "And as the ships tossed to and fro, men's stomachs began to feel a qualm, until this feeling of sickness made them insensible to danger."

Richard's mission to take Jerusalem from Saladin did not prevent him from romance on the way. He landed on Cyprus and conquered it, and while there married Berengaria of Navarre, who had come with him from Europe. He went on to attack Acre, a port on the coast of Palestine (1191). It was here that Philip Augustus quarreled with Richard, left the crusade and returned to France, claiming to be sick. Frederick Barbarossa, who had planned to join forces with them in Acre, had drowned while crossing a river in Cicilia as he journeyed by land.

Richard was now left alone to fight the Moslems. His fame was known to them. They spoke of him as a king "of mighty strength, vast courage, and firm will." His very name inspired terror in the East, for all had heard of his great personal strength and of his ruthlessness toward those who stood in his way. But he failed to do what Godfrey had done for two reasons: After some battles he fell ill and could no longer lead his troops, and his opponent, Saladin, was also a great warrior and leader.

Saladin

Saladin was as chivalrous as any Western knight. In the last battle that Richard fought with him, Richard's horse was killed and he started to fight on foot. Saladin sent him a fresh steed. In Richard's illness, a fever, Saladin sent him snow from the mountains with pears, peaches, and other fruits for a cooling drink. Saladin also defended Jerusalem as a Holy City, "in that it was the place whence our Prophet made his journey by night to Heaven and is destined to be the gathering place of our nation on the last day."

The best Richard could accomplish was a three-year truce, in which Jerusalem remained in the hands of Saladin, but both Moslems and Christians were allowed to visit their shrines in peace and safety.

Richard sailed for home and his ship was wrecked in the Adriatic, so he had to continue by land. He was captured by an adversary in Austria and imprisoned in a castle. His brother, Prince John, had tried to take power while Richard was away and formed a plot against him. Richard's whereabouts were unknown. Blondel, his minstrel, was said to have found him by traveling through Europe and singing near all the great castles. Richard heard him and made himself known. He was freed by ransom and returned to England but died soon after.

In all, there were five crusades as well as a "children's crusade" led by Stephen, a French shepherd lad, and Nicholas, a young German. The children sought to reach the Holy Land in order to convert the infidels, but all of them perished or were sold into slavery by their captors. This was in the year 1212. In 1229 King Frederick II of Germany made a treaty with the Sultan of Egypt, crowned himself King of Jerusalem, and made ten years of peace, after which Jerusalem was lost again. In 1248 King Louis of France and Prince Edward of England both tried to overcome the Turks and failed. In 1291 the last of the Franks left the East and the age of the Crusades came to an end.

The Hospitalers and the Templars

Before the First Crusade a certain association of monks maintained hospitals in which to care for pilgrims who were ill. They also donned armor and came to the aid of pilgrims who were under attack. They were called the Knights Hospitaller. Thus as both knights and monks their order grew, many noble knights joining it, and in 1113 it was transformed into a military order, "The Knights Hospitaller of St. John," while it continued to care for the sick. Its fame increased and much land and wealth was given to the Hospitalers in the East and West. They built many fortified monasteries in the Holy Land, still to be seen today. When the Europeans left the Holy Land after the Crusades, the Hospitalers moved their headquarters to the Isle of Rhodes and later to Malta. This order still exists and its emblem is the Maltese Cross.

In 1119, after the First Crusade, a group of eight French knights banded together to defend pilgrims from the attacks of Moslems. Their headquarters was in the King's palace on or near the site of Solomon's Temple, and they  came to be called the Templars. They took vows of obedience, poverty and purity, just as if they were monks, and they wore white cloaks adorned with a red cross over their armor. A Templar might never refuse to fight, even if he were only one against several, and he might never ask for mercy. As the fame of the Templars spread, many nobles joined the order, renouncing all their wealth and lands to "serve Christ." This wealth and property fell to the Order of the Templars, which became immensely rich and powerful in Europe, to which it had spread. The Order flourished for forty years or more, but after the Crusades it was dissolved by King Philip IV of France with the aid of Pope Clement VI. Two reasons are given for this: King Philip, who was in need of money, wanted to get hold of their wealth; and they practiced secret rites which were not approved by the Roman Church.

The Results of the Crusades

Many crusaders became colonists in the Holy Land. The feudal lords built their castles and had their domains for many a year along the coast of Palestine. Merchants from the Italian cities of Genoa, Venice, and Pisa had sent supplies in their ships to help the crusaders. They always made sure that they were well paid and, when they had aided the successful siege of a town, claimed a quarter in the town where they might have their market, docks, church, and all that was necessary for a permanent center for their commerce. This district then belonged to the town from which the merchants came. The towns sent their own governors to rule these market places. Thus trade began to flourish between East and West. Silks, spices, camphor, musk, pearls, and ivory were brought by the Mohammedans to the commercial vendors of Palestine and Syria and, through Italian merchants, found their way to Germany, France, and England.

During feudal times in Europe, the first traders were peddlers, craftsmen who, carrying products of their own making in packs on their backs, went from place to place to sell their wares. As they prospered, they banded together, won protection from the feudal lords, built their burghs or villages close to the castle walls, and increased production of their various crafts in order to do more trading. They took their products to trade fairs, traveling along the river valleys, meeting other traders from the south and from the east. Trading towns were built up where the trade routes crossed, where water travel ceased and land travel started, or where boats unloaded their cargoes along the coasts or up the rivers. As trade flourished, these commercial towns grew independent of feudal protection. And as merchants with goods from the East invaded Europe, the manor system disappeared. The trade centers to the north included Paris, Cologne, Hamburg, Lubeck, and Bremen, and to the south Barcelona, Cadiz, and Toledo. The trade routes made a network over the face of the land with at least 35 town springing up as centers for traders.

The European world now began to open up not only to goods but to culture from the East. Thousands of the European peoples, who had never before been far from their little hamlets or great castles, had now as crusaders been to the ends of the earth, so to speak, and had seen much that they had never before imagined: great cities and seaports, and people who knew more than they did, namely the Arabs. And so, much of Arab science, hitherto limited to the Moorish realms in Spain and Sicily, now made its way to other parts of Europe.

The Streams of
Human Development

All during the Middle Ages, several streams in the course of the development of the human being were in opposition:
- » The Popes seek absolute power.
- » The Emperors vie for independence from the Popes.
- » The Merchants in the cities and towns try to win wealth and freedom for themselves.
- » The German nobles try to be independent of the Emperor, using the Pope's favor to gain their ends.
- » The Hohenstaufen dynasty brings a new impulse: Frederick I, his son Henry VI, and Frederick II, son of Henry.

The antagonists of this century in Germany were the Welfs and the Hohenstaufens, two princely houses. The Welfs had a following among those nobles who tried to maintain independent feudal states. The Hohenstaufens had the impulse toward order, culture, power, and the authority of an emperor over the quarrelsome German nobles. Later these two parties came to be called the Guelphs and the Ghibellines (Italian terms).

In Lombardy, northern Italy, there were many towns like Milan, Verona, and Cremona, which were practically independent states governed by rich citizens and nobles. They had fortified palaces in the towns, for they often had to defend themselves from the poor, who revolted because they didn't have any voice in government, and from each other in their quarrels for wealth and power. These towns, however, became wealthy due to the merchants, and they opposed paying taxes to a German emperor. They united with each other in "The Lombard League."

- » The Papal State, north and northeast of Rome, was ruled by the Popes, who began to act like kings in search of political and worldly power.
- » In Southern Italy and Sicily, what was known as the Kingdom of Sicily (or of Naples) was in the hands of Norman kings at this time.
- » The Hohenstaufens were the outstanding figures of this period and represented a new impulse.

FREDERICK I (Barbarossa)
Ruled 1152–1190

Frederick Barbarossa (Red Beard) was elected by German nobles as Emperor and was crowned in Charlemagne's church at Aachen. He informed the Pope, saying, "The headship of the Empire has been bestowed on me by God." He did not ask the Pope's sanction as his predecessors had done.

As emperor Frederick faced three challenges, and he gave his efforts to dealing with them: to subdue the rebellious vassals in Germany (the Welfs); to maintain his imperial authority against the opposition of the Popes; to retain power over the towns of Northern Italy. In the second and third efforts he failed. The Pope was on the side of the towns and was the feudal lord of Naples and Sicily where the Norman kings were his vassals. But Frederick married his son, Henry, to Costanza, the heiress of Sicily and the daughter of King Roger, the Norman.

As to the first challenge, Frederick spent forty years fighting in Germany and Italy without bringing the struggle to any real conclusion. His followers and enemies, alike, regarded him as a great leader. The Germans looked forward to the House of Hohenstaufen being rulers of a future great and peaceful kingdom. Then Barbarossa, at age 70, went to the Crusades, took part in many skirmishes, and lost his life.

When he did not return, the legend arose that he did not die but only withdrew from the world to a mountain cave in Austria (at Untersberg near Salzburg), where he still sleeps on a rocky throne. Nearby, a dead pear tree will blossom, and on that day Barbarossa will awake, come forth, hang his shield on the tree, and commence a tremendous battle in which the whole world will join, and the good shall overcome the wicked.

HENRY VI
Ruled 1192–1197

When we speak of the greatness of the Hohenstaufen Emperors, we can mean only Frederick I and Frederick II. We cannot include Henry, who now claimed the Kingdom of Sicily, but had to establish his claim by force of arms, even though he had been crowned by the Pope, and even though the land was the realm of his wife, Costanza. Her nephew, Tancred, had taken the throne, but died, leaving it to a younger son, William. Henry took the throne from him easily, opened the tomb of Tancred, stripped the body of its royal robes, pursued William, had him blinded, and sent him with his mother and sisters into captivity in Germany. Then Henry took possession of the gold and silver ornaments of ancient Norman kings and transported them to Germany. Loaded with this treasure, 160 animals moved it to his castle on the Rhine. He also caused rebellious Sicilian nobles to be blinded, made them sit on seats of red-hot iron and put crowns of hot iron on their heads. This example forced all others in Sicily to submit to him, but also led his wife to hate him and all Germans.

As Emperor, Henry bargained with the Pope, promising to give him all lands belonging to the clergy in return for the Pope's promise that the Crown and the Throne would become hereditary in the Hohenstaufen family. He also promised the German princes that their sons might inherit their lands, thus returning to them much that his father had made part of the kingdom and breaking up the unity which his father had tried to win in Germany.

In the year 1197, after only six years as emperor, while on a hunting trip in Lombardy, Henry VI caught cold, developed a severe illness, and died, leaving his wife, Costanza, and his three-year-old son, Frederick, in Palermo, Sicily. His death caused as much excitement as an earthquake. Enemies saw a chance. In Germany quarrels broke out about the throne between the Welfs and the Hohenstaufens.

FREDERICK II
Ruled 1212–1250

Frederick II was born on December 26, 1194, in Jesi, Apulia. He was a Christmas child. In Germany he would have been called a "Baldur." He later called his birthplace his "Bethlehem." The year after Henry's death, Innocent III became Pope and Costanza granted him guardianship over her son. Innocent became Frederick's greatest enemy.

Costanza died shortly after Henry, and Frederick became dependent on the Pope, who wanted him to become the King of Sicily but nothing more. The Pope appointed a Welf named Otto as King of Germany. Otto promised the Pope all he asked. After being crowned, Otto broke his promises and tried to win the power he had agreed to forgo. The Pope announced, "I am sorry I have brought Otto to power."

Although under the Pope's protection, Frederick did not receive his care, but grew up in Palermo under the care of various burghers who took turns as his guardians. Frederick had a hard time. Again and again people tried to do away with him. Here, in a town full of all kinds of traders, sailors, scholars from the East, and in a country not long since a part of the Saracen empire, Frederick grew up almost wild. Yet he received a most excellent education from some teachers not known historically, but it is certain that they were Arabic.

The boy showed kingly poise and a ruling nature, for he was obstinate and would act only out of his own will. His feeling for right and wrong amazed people. He had a strong body and was well-trained in the use of varied weapons, was a perfect hunter, was never tired, was constantly in motion, and worked late into the night.

At the age of 12 he wanted to get rid of his guardian, the Pope. At 14 he became of age and the Pope had to release him. Shortly after Frederick became independent, he came into conflict with the Pope and opposed a new archbishop's appointment in Palermo. The Pope demanded obedience. Frederick was still in constant danger of his life, for he was known throughout the Empire by both friends and enemies of his grandfather's house.

In 1211 the Germans who had been quarreling under Otto deposed him, and the Council of German nobles offered Frederick the crown, saying, "We look upon you as the one who seems most able. Although you are young in years, you are old in wisdom. Nature has bestowed on you the most noble gifts."

Frederick accepted and set out for Germany. He was 18 years old. He had no money, so he stopped in Rome and saw Innocent III for the first time, and asked for his help. He had to take the oath of fealty as vassal to the Pope and thus gained the Pope's sanction.

From Rome onward his life was endangered by lurking enemies. His companions deserted him, and he made his way almost alone over the Alps to Konstanz, Germany. There he found that Otto had regained power. The Bishop of Konstanz sided with Otto and refused to admit Frederick into the town. Bishop Berard, Frederick's companion, then announced that the Pope had excommunicated Otto, and Frederick was admitted to Konstanz. A whirlwind of acclaim rose from the people when they saw him, and the name passed from one to another: "our Wonder Child."

Frederick was crowned King of the Germans in July, 1215. He was 21 years old. To the astonishment of the clerics, at this moment of coronation, he stood at the tomb of Charlemagne and "took the Cross," vowed a crusade, declaring that as a Christian he would give, with a pure heart, his body and his mind to God as truly as if in a burnt sacrifice on the fire of the altar.

When the Pope heard of this, he called a council of churchmen in Rome and made his statement that the Church, as the greatest power, was the one to declare crusades. Said the Pope, "All power is from God. The Pope is the mediator between God and human beings. The Pope is less than God but more than man. In us God is honored, and if one dishonors the Pope, then one dishonors God." Pope Innocent was at the end of his life, and Frederick was at the beginning of his.

Frederick stayed five years in Germany, established his rule well, then returned to Rome. He brought gold to the Pope, held his stirrup, led his horse a few paces, (all signs of his vassalage), then mounted his own horse and rode to his coronation in Rome as Emperor. A new crusade was planned between the Pope and the Emperor as a crusade of the Church.

Frederick returned to Sicily after having been away for eight years. He had left it as a poor boy and now returned as a powerful Emperor. He set to work at once to reorganize the kingdom of Sicily and made of it the kind of state that is to be found only hundreds of years later in other lands. He made just laws and laws against gambling and other vices, gave castles and lands to men of ability, and developed fleets of merchants, ships, and warships. Trade increased the wealth of the kingdom. Scholars and thinkers flocked to his court, some of whom translated Aristotle from Arabic into Latin.

Frederick presented the translation to the University of Bologna with these words, "Science must go hand in hand with government, legislation, and the pursuits of war. From youth upward we have sought and loved science, whereby the soul of man becomes enlightened and strengthened, and without which his life is deprived of all regulation and innate freedom."

> » He was a renowned falconer and made a study of birds; he wrote a book on details of their habits and anatomy still referred to by naturalists today.

From *The Book of Falconry* by Frederick II

- » Attending his court was his animal collection, like a circus or zoo, with great pomp!
- » He knew Greek, Latin, Italian, French, German, and Arabic. He composed poems, but also excelled in all physical powers (warlike and bodily exercises).
- » He founded a university at Naples in 1224, sponsored a medical school at Salerno, and established art museums.

He was able to gather around him the most celebrated men of the age without any feeling of jealousy toward them. His friend, the Sultan of Egypt, sent him a gift, a model of the sun and moon revolving so as to show the hours of day and night "in just and exact relation."

In all this time as emperor, Frederick had ignored the agreement with the Pope to make a crusade. In 1225 he made a new agreement with a new Pope, Honorius, who made him sign a written promise to start a crusade in 1227: If he didn't go, Frederick was to pay the Pope 100,000 pieces of gold and be excommunicated. Frederick, however, sought freedom from all ties with the papacy and did not go. Honorius died in 1227, and Pope Gregory IX excommunicated Frederick, forbidding him to go on a crusade. In defiance and to show his independence from papal control, Frederick then went, in 1228.

He went, knowing that the Lombards were intending to invade Sicily. He reached Jerusalem safely, made a treaty with the Saracen ruler, in which Jerusalem, Bethlehem, and Nazareth were given back to the Christians, and then he went back to the Temple of the Holy Sepulcher and crowned himself "King of Jerusalem" as all clerics had been forbidden to do so. All this he accomplished between a Saturday and a Monday and sailed right back to Sicily, where the Lombards had started trouble. He turned back their invasion. The Pope had to withdraw the excommunication and make a truce with Frederick, who now had four titles: King of Germany, King of Sicily, King of Jerusalem, and Emperor of Rome.

Frederick considered himself as the bringer of world peace. As the Lombards were disturbing the peace, he fought them. The Pope was supporting the Lombards. The Pope had now sworn the defeat of the Hohenstaufen and did all in his power to bring it about. He spoke, later, of Frederick II as "the Anti-Christ." He asked from Frederick unconditional submission to the Pope.

But Frederick entered and defeated Lombardy. He was now at the peak of his power, and strangely, at this time, he knighted Rudolf of Hapsburg who became Emperor after Frederick's death. Now he set out to conquer Rome and declare himself as the follower of Caesar Augustus. Soon ill-luck overtook him. Milan and five other cities opposed him, and his troops had to withdraw. His son, Konrad, came to his aid with troops from Germany, but without success.

The Pope roused a lot of people against Frederick. There were two parties to the conflict. The Ghibellines were the Emperor's followers; the Guelfs were the Pope's. The Emperor was again excommunicated, in 1239, and the Pope tried to overthrow him and invade Sicily with the help of the people of Genoa and Venice. Frederick defeated them.

In 1241 Frederick went to Rome, and was at its portals when the Pope called upon Saints Peter and Paul to save Rome, since the Romans were unwilling to do so. This roused the Romans to defend the city, and the Emperor passed it by to go toward northern Italy. On Frederick's next approach to Rome, Pope Gregory died.

The search for a new pope lasted for nearly a year, and Frederick influenced the choice of a friend of his, who became Innocent IV. However, Innocent IV became Frederick's adversary, calling a council in Lyons and in 1245 declaring the dethronement of Frederick. Yet this Pope did not return to Rome, out of fear.

The Emperor then wrote to the European kings and noblemen, "It was always our will and our intention that the clerics should remain what they were in the original church, leading a devotional life, because such people are able to see the angels and they can have a wondrous halo around them. They can heal the sick, can awaken the dead, and, through their holiness, they have power over kings and nobles but not through external weapons."

Continuing his fight against Frederick, Pope Innocent IV influenced many, including one of Frederick's sons, and the Emperor again had to be alert for attacks on his life.

The Pope's council in Lyons elected a new German Emperor, Henry Raspé, but who died soon after. When Frederick declared he would go to Lyons, the Pope was in distress. Events interfered. Enemies burned Parma, and Frederick lost 1500 men. Mishaps occurred one after another. Towns revolted. His son, Enzio, was captured and imprisoned until his death 23 years later.

In December 1250, while on a hunting trip, Frederick caught a fever and died on December 13th. Archbishop Berard was with him and gave him the last rites. Manfred, Frederick's youngest son, buried his father in Palermo. Said another son, Konrad, "The sun of the world has set, the sun of the right, the preserver of peace."

Now the Pope sent out the order: "Destroy the House of Hohenstaufen completely." His agent was a man of cruelty, Charles of Anjou, who did not rest until all of Frederick's sons were either imprisoned or put to death. Three grandsons were put in a dungeon, in chains, as small boys, where they were to remain half-naked, ill-fed, and untaught for 31 years. The last Hohenstaufen was beheaded in 1268.

Powers of the Roman Church

The Roman Church reached the height of its power in the 12th and 13th centuries. This medieval church was different from the churches today. Everyone was required to belong to it. To refuse allegiance to it, to question its authority or teachings, was regarded as treason against God, punishable by death. It was a rich institution, had vast territories and many vassals from whom it received revenues, and everyone as well had to pay tithes (taxes).

It was no longer merely a religious body, although of course it conducted services, built cathedrals, administered the sacraments, and so on. But it was also a state and as such had its own code of laws and its own courts in which it tried many cases of the kind which are now settled in civil courts, cases concerning marriage, wills, sworn contracts, and usury, blasphemy, sorcery, and heresy. The Church even had its own prisons.

The Pope, as head of the Church State, controlled every churchman in every Christian country. He made the laws and saw to it that they were observed. Dispensations, that is, exceptions allowed in regard to merely human laws, were given for good reasons, for example permission for cousins to marry, or freeing a monk from his vows; but scriptural, or divine, laws were not set aside.

The Pope's ambassadors to every country were called his legates. They carried the rule of the Pope to distant parts. One legate absolved all subjects of King John of England from their oath of fealty to him. This was at the time when they refused to fight for his lands in France.

The Church government had to have many officials for the papal *curia*, or court, in Rome. To carry on this government the Pope needed money. He charged high fees for those who brought cases to court and high fees to bishops or archbishops as the price of their election, sometimes one-half of their first year's income.

The archbishops were in control of the bishops. The bishops, as heads of their own bishoprics around the chief cathedrals, had vassals and subvassals, but were often vassals themselves to the king or neighboring lords. The parish priests, under the bishops, were poor and propertyless and served the people in the parish churches, conducted services, marriage ceremonies, baptisms, and funerals.

Penances were punishments for sins and were meted out by the priests, such as fasting, repetition of prayers, visits to holy places, abstinence from one's usual amusements. A journey to the Holy Land took the place of all other penance. Gradually the Church became willing to accept money in place of penance.

The Churchmen were the only educated persons. All teachers were of the clergy. All books were written by the clergy and by monks. All public documents and proclamations of the Kings were written by the clergy. "The priests and monks held the pen for the King." But all church offices were open to all ranks of men and were not hereditary.

The Church could cast out its enemies by excommunication and forbid all men to associate with them. By interdict it could suspend all religious services in a whole city or country, and so impose its will over nations.

The Churchmen held the keys to the Kingdom of Heaven and without their aid no one could hope to enter in. But Christ had said to the people, "The Kingdom of Heaven is within you."

and

"How hard is it for them that trust in riches to enter into the Kingdom of God! It is easier for a camel to go through the eye of a needle than for a rich man to enter the Kingdom of God."

In the long struggle between popes and emperors, the emperors were finally worsted.

The Towns

The Church now stood between the people and the Kingdom of Heaven, as if it were guarding the gates and charging admission. The Church was rich and powerful, but a class of people was also emerging to become rich and powerful.

We know about their beginnings. The first of them were peddlers, craftsmen who carried products of their own making in backpacks and went from town to town to sell their wares. As they prospered, they banded together as traders and won protection from the feudal lords, built their burghs close to castle walls, and took their wares to fairs, traveling along the river valleys. Trading towns sprang up where the trade routes crossed.

Venice, Naples, Pisa, Genoa, Marseilles, Barcelona, Lisbon, Milan, Verona, Lyons, Paris, Nuremberg, Antwerp, Bremen, Hamburg—all developed as commercial towns. As trade flourished from the time of the crusades, these towns flourished and no longer clung to castle walls. As the merchants with goods from the East invaded Europe, the manor system disappeared. Craftsmen aimed to make a surplus for trade. Northern products were carried south, eastern products were taken north. New crafts were developed. The Venetians learned how to make silk. Parisians wove tapestries, imitating the Saracens.

There was little money from the few gold and silver mines in western Europe. The people took to "clipping," paring off a little of the precious metal before passing money on (hence the irregular edges of old coins). The "just price" was merely enough to cover the cost of materials and labor; it was considered outrageous to ask for more than this, no matter how anxious the purchaser might be to have the article and thus offer more for it.

Manufacturing and trading were carried on by the same people. They had to sell directly to consumers in their own town-market and could not, elsewhere, sell a whole stock to a dealer who might then raise the just price for his own benefit.

Money could not be bought and sold, that is, "charged for." Interest (usury) was considered wicked, since in charging interest for loans, one man would be taking advantage of another's shortcomings or troubles. The Church condemned usurers to non-Christian burials and their wills were annulled. Money lending was left to the Jews, from whom Christian conduct was not expected; thus this became a Jewish business in which the practice of usury was allowed. Kings and nobles borrowed large sums at high rates, sometimes 46% in England.

The traders had their problems with tolls and duties levied by lords and churchmen through whose territories they had to travel. For example:

- » A certain monastery, lying between Paris and the sea, required fishermen, who were hurrying with fresh fish to the city, to stop and let the monks pick out fresh fish worth the three-pence toll. After sorting and handling, the remaining fish were thus left in poor condition.
- » Wine boats traveling up the Seine to Paris had to be boarded by the agent of a certain Lord, who could open three casks, taste wine from each, and then claim a measure from the one he liked best.

Sea trade flourished in spite of storms, rocky coasts with no lighthouses, pirates (often men of high rank), and false signals from shore or other ships luring vessels to be wrecked by "wreckers" who then plundered them. Thus there developed the "fleet" of merchant ships traveling together under the protection of a man-of-war.

The commercial towns, at first independent, began to form leagues for mutual defense. Lubeck, the northernmost German port, became the leader in the Hanseatic League of 70 towns who made war on pirates and even on kings who interfered with their interests.

Thus, trade was not as yet carried on between nations but between towns. Merchants carried on their business as members of the merchants' guilds in their towns under the protection of treaties arranged by the towns. If a merchant from London failed to pay a debt in Hamburg, and another Londoner happened to pass through Hamburg in the meantime, he might be lawfully seized and held in Hamburg till the debt was paid. There was no national identity; a man from London was as much a foreigner in Bristol as would be one from Cologne or Antwerp.

The craft guilds were as important as the merchants' guilds and protected the interests of the craftsmen, who now increased in number as a separate group from the merchants. "The butchers, the bakers, the candlestick makers," each craft was carefully regulated so that not too many would crowd in. Apprentices spent three to ten years, without wages, learning a trade. For goldsmiths it was ten years. Journeymen worked for wages under master workmen for several more years. The number of apprentices to each master was limited to prevent too many journeymen. Working hours were limited each day. No man was allowed to take on more work than his fellow members. As youngsters many serfs joined the guilds, thus bringing an end to serfdom. The townsmen found freedom from the lords, tendering money payments instead of services. Wealth increased freedom! But watchtowers were built to guard the freedom, and a guard was on watch day and night to ring the bell in the belfry in the case of approaching danger. The building from which the tower rose was the town hall, containing an assembly room for the town's leaders and a prison.

Commercial towns, the cathedral towns, and the castle villages were the three symbols of the developing civilization of Europe in the 12th–14th centuries.

Waldensians and Albigensians

Among the townspeople in France there were some who did not submit to the power of the Church. They continued to accept the Christian faith but refused to obey the clergy.

The Waldensians were the followers of Peter Waldo (1140–1218), a wealthy merchant of Lyons, who gave all his wealth to the needy. His followers took a vow of poverty. They went about teaching about Christ and explaining the scriptures, which they translated from Latin into the language of the people. Waldo and his followers were called "the Poor Men of Lyons." At first they had not the intention to break away from the Church, but they were denounced as heretics and driven from the city. This was about the time of the coronation of Frederick II in Aachen. For hundreds of years to come, the Waldensians were considered enemies of the Church.

The Albigensians, people of the town of Albi in southern France, likewise ignored the Church, claiming that their religion was older than Christianity and that it also contained Christianity. They, like the Persians of ancient times from whose mysteries they might well have drawn, believed in the forces of light as forces of good, in darkness as the realm of evil, and that light and darkness, good and evil, were constantly at war with each other, forever fighting for victory in the universe. They proclaimed that Christ was of the light, but that the Church represented the power of evil. They too were condemned as heretics, and Pope Innocent III sent a crusade against them in 1208. This crusade was the cause of one of the bloodiest wars in Europe. Not only were the Albigensians destroyed, but the local towns and farms were laid waste and burned in barbarous fashion.

The Holy Inquisition was a system of courts and spies set up by the Church to ferret out heretics. It did not help for a suspected heretic to deny it, for it was assumed that any criminal denies his guilt. His true state was judged by incidents such as: an accidental conversation with another heretic; unintentional lack of respect toward Church affairs; malicious testimony by one's neighbors. If a suspect confessed his guilt, he was forgiven and readmitted to the Church but usually received a penance of life imprisonment. If a suspect refused to admit guilt, he was turned over to the King's court, where he would usually be condemned to be burned alive without further trial.

The Waldensians and Albigensians tried to live worthily in spite of the Church.

There was yet another group forming within the Church. Its founder was the son of a well-to-do merchant in Assisi, a little town in central Italy. His name was Francis, and he was to be a true follower of Christ and to keep many people, who would otherwise revolt, close to the Christian faith in its origins.

Francis of Assisi

Before Frederick II was crowned, and while Innocent III was still the Pope, there came to him one day a young Italian, Francis of Assisi, and with Francis were a dozen others. All were dressed in gray, like peasants, and they were barefoot. They asked the Pope for permission to live in the world as monks without possessions, without even a monastery, among the poor and the sick. They were determined to carry out Christ's instructions to his twelve apostles, "to preach the Gospel, to heal the sick, to take nothing for their journey, neither staves, nor scrip, nor bread, nor money, to have neither shoes nor two coats apiece."

Pope Innocent hesitated. He did not believe that anyone could lead a life of absolute poverty, and he was concerned that in their way of life these men would put to shame the rich and comfortable of the clergy at that time. Yet he knew that if he didn't grant their request, it would look like he disapproved of Christ's teachings. He finally gave his approval; and in the following years people in many lands saw with wonder the arrival of the "Franciscans," barefooted, in patched gowns or habits with ropes for belts around their waists, who followed a Christlike way of life, taking no thought for themselves, but following a rule of poverty and of service to others.

For 25 years, until his death in 1226, the followers of Francis of Assisi increased to several thousands. Wherever they went, they comforted the people and preached the gospel so that many who doubted the holiness of the bishops and archbishops nevertheless followed these friars with great devotion and love.

Francis was born c. 1181 in Assisi. He was named John by his mother, but his father changed the name to Francis. As a rich young man he was welcomed among young nobles. He loved fine clothes, loved to spend money, and took part in knightly adventures. In one adventure, a quarrel between the young knights of Assisi and those of another town, the former were taken as prisoners for a year. After their release, a more serious war started between the towns.

Francis dreamed of a great palace full of weapons and told himself, "This is a sign that I should be a soldier." On his way to battle he heard a voice saying, "Go no further. You have wrongly understood the dream. Go back to Assisi and hear the right meaning."

At home, the voice then said, "The weapons in your dream are of mercy, kindness, and love, which you must wield to help your fellow men."

It is also told that he had a long illness between the time he was a carefree, young noble and the time he became a friar. It was after this illness that his friends noticed a change in him and asked him if he was in love. "Yes," he said, "but I shall marry a fairer and nobler bride than you ever saw, who shall surpass all others in beauty and excel them in wisdom." He named her Lady Poverty. He then began to go among the poor, especially helping and comforting the lepers. Leprosy was a disease that was considered, at that time, "unclean." The sufferers were shunned and abhorred.

Francis's father had no use for his son's ideas and one day threatened to disinherit him. Francis cheerfully took off his rich clothes, put on the gray cloak of his father's gardener, and left home to continue his visits to the poor.

His first follower was another rich young man of Assisi, who sold all his property and gave the money to the poor. Others soon joined these two. In their poverty and homelessness, Francis and his Brothers were always so joyous that they were known as the Jongleurs of God. From the Franciscans people learned that those who serve God are filled with joy of heart, that only those in whom the Devil has a seat are sad.

Full of love for man and beast, Francis especially loved birds. In the last years of his life, he became almost blind. When the hour of his death approached, he asked to be taken from the rich house of the Bishop of Assisi, where he was being cared for, to the little chapel which he had considered as his only home after leaving his father's house. There, it is said, at the hour of his death, the swallows swarmed about the eaves of the chapel, singing as if their hearts would break.

St. Francis Talking to the Birds

The Hundred Years' War and Jeanne D'Arc

Since the time of Edward III, the English kings had laid claim to the throne of France. Edward had started what was to be a warfare that continued off and on for one hundred years (1346–1450) on French soil. These wars consisted of battles, most of which the English won with the advantage of their style of weapons that were long bows. A long bow was made the height of the man who used it, with steel-pointed arrows that could be shot at a hundred yards and penetrate the armor of both knights and horses. The English occupied parts of France and captured the French king at one time. Truces were made, but "free companies" of French and English were disinclined to settle down, and they raided the countryside in search of plunder. Little by little the country districts were invaded much like the barbarians of old.

Petrarch, an Italian poet and scholar, described France during these years:

> I could not believe this was the same France which I had seen so rich and flourishing. Nothing presented itself to my eyes but a fearful solitude, and utter poverty, land uncultivated, houses in ruins. Even the neighborhood of Paris showed everywhere marks of desolation and conflagration. The streets are deserted, the roads overgrown with weeds, the whole is a vast solitude.

Yet, the towns, on the whole, took little part in this and carried on business as if no warfare were going on around them.

By 1430 the English had conquered all of France north of the River Loire, including Normandy. Charles, heir to the throne of France, was in the south, weak and indolent, enjoying the life of his court and not opposing the English.

The English were besieging Orleans when a young maid appeared at the court to offer herself as a leader of the forces of France. "Gentle Dauphin, my name is Jeanne the Maid. The Heavenly King sends me to tell you that you shall be anointed and crowned at Rheims, and you shall be lieutenant of the Heavenly King, who is the King of France."

Jeanne the Maid

Three years before Henry V of England won his victory over the French at Agincourt, this maid had been born in Domrémy in Lorraine (1412). She was now about 18 years old. Her name was Jeanne D'Arc.

She grew up in a religious home, hearing of the wars and the wasted land in France, hearing the tramp of passing troops, and was filled with pity and sorrow. When she was 13 years old, and the English were again invading, she sat under a tree and had a vision of St. Michael surrounded by angels and other Saints, and heard their voices telling her to go to the Dauphin (Charles) to help him recover his realm. After this vision she said she wept because she wanted them to take her with them. She told her father of the voices. He said he'd rather she drown than go on such an errand. By the time she was 17 years old, her voices had won.

While the English were storming Orleans, she went alone to the castle of a neighboring lord and persuaded him to take her to the King. Although many were amazed, doubtful, even scornful, Jeanne won the King and, dressed in armor, led the French against the English. The siege of Orleans was raised and after certain other victories, Jeanne led the Dauphin to Rheims and stood

Section of frieze depicting the "The Life of Joan of Arc"

beside him as he was crowned Charles VII, King of France. Now she wanted to go home. The King begged her further aid.

In defensive battle at Compiégne against the Duke of Burgundy, who was in the pay of the English, she was captured by a Burgundian soldier, and the Duke sold her to the English for 1000 pounds.

The English were afraid of her influence. Clerics tried her as a witch, to try to get her to admit that her voices were of the Devil, and tried her as a heretic. Worn out by days of questioning, she weakened and admitted this. Life imprisonment was the sentence. Then her courage returned and she denied her confession. She was turned over to soldiers who burned her as a heretic on May 29, 1431. As the flames rose around her, she asked for a Cross. A soldier tied together two sticks of wood and gave them to her. When all was over, an English soldier whispered to a companion, "We are lost. We have burned a saint."

The English had no further successes. By 1453 they were driven out of all of France except Calais, which they kept until 1558.

Attributes

*All illustrations are in either the public domain
or licenced under Creative Commons, Wikipedia.*

p9	(left) SeaWiFS (NASA) collected this view of the Arabian Peninsula and of dust blowing across the Persian Gulf, 2008 (right) View of the Iberian Peninsula; Suomi NPP VIIRS data through NASA Worldview, Pierre Marcuse, 2019
p18	Mohammed Ben Abdallah, V. Zweig
p25	Incomplete text from the Holy Quran, inscribed by Ali, the fourth Caliph of Islam, National Museum, New Delhi
p28	Tāriq ibn Ziyād: illustration intended for the mid-19th-century history of the European Middle Ages, Theodor Hosemann (1807–1875)
p31	(top) Imaginary sketch representing Abbasid Caliph Hārūn al-Rashid (bottom) Imaginary drawing of Abbasid caliph Abdullah al-Ma'mūn. Both images scanned from a book entitled *Kitāb khizānat al-ayyām fī tarājim al-'izām*, first published in New York (1899)
p33	(left) Illustration from *One Thousand and One Arabian Nights*, "Tale of the Tailor": "So I bade the page open the box and the Barber laid down the astrolabe…and, sitting on the ground, turned over the scents and incense and aloes-wood and essences till I was well-nigh distraught." Albert Letchford (1866–1905) (right) Astrolabe at Bank Negara Malaysia Museum and Art Gallery (photograph, Wee Hong)
p38	Pépin III, dit Le Bref, Roi des Francs, from Portraits of the Kings of France, Palace of Versailles, Louis-Félix Amiel (1802–1864)
p39	Charlemagne, from the collection of Portraits of Kings of France 1837–1838, Musée Historique de Versailles, Louis-Félix Amiel
p53	*La Chanson de Roland,* [*Song of Roland*], 11e édition, frontispiece, Léon Gautier (1832–1897)
p54	Carisbrooke Castle gatehouse, looking in from the east, Isle of Wight (1464)
p55	View of the Castle of Zafra
p56	Castell Beaumaris, Ynys Môn (Anglesey), Wales (photograph 44, Llywelyn2000)
p59	*Franciscan Monks in the Cloister of Santa Maria in Ara Coeli*, Rome
p62	Scriptorium: Scribe working on a manuscript, surrounded by his research material, Jean Le Tavernier (–1462), Bibliothèque Nationale de France, Paris
p63	(top) Speyer Cathedral, Germany [photograph Friedrich Haag] (bottom) East window in Carlisle Cathedral, one of the finest examples of Flowing Decorated Gothic tracery in England. The glass of the tracery is Medieval and the lights is Victorian; Carlisle, UK.
p64	Porto Cathedral, Portugal, side view [photograph, Ivan Stesso]
p65	(top) Gregory VII: from *The Lives and Times of the Popes* by Artaud de Montor (1772–1849), New York: The Catholic Publication Society of America, 1911. It was originally published in 1842. (bottom) Henry IV, British School (before 1626), Dulwich Picture Gallery, London, Google Art Project

p72	Howard Pyle illustration from the 1903 edition of *The Story of King Arthur and His Knights*; scanned and archived at http://www.gallery.oldbookart.com/main.php?g2_itemId=2708
p73	Illustration by Paul Mercuri from *Costumes Historiques* (Paris, c. 1850s or 1860s)
p74	Portrait of Alfred the Great, after a painting in the Bodleian Library, colour engraving by English School, 19th century
p76	Edward the Confessor in the Wilton Diptych, 1395–1399, National Gallery, London
p77	Portrait of William the Conqueror, artist unknown, circa 1620, National Portrait Gallery, London
p79	(top) Medieval statue (1370–1380) of Thomas à Becket in former Cistercian monastery for nuns in Sankt Thomas, Germany (bottom) King Richard I, British (English) School, 1620, National Trust Collection, UK
p84	*Peter the Hermit and Alexius Comnenus*, 19th century painting, Palace of Versailles
p87	A romantic 19th century vision of Godfrey of Bouillon and leaders of the First Crusade, Alphonse-Marie-Adolphe de Neuville (1836–1885)
p89	*Richard the Lion Heart on His Way to Jerusalem*, James William Glass, circa 1850
p90	Sultan Selahaddin Eyyubi El Kurdi Saladin, Sultan of Egypt and Syria, print, Austrian National Library, Jerôme David, 1650, public domain Mark 1.0
p92	Knights Templar, artist unknown (1870), in Munich Picture Book; no further information provided
p96	Emperor Frederick I, known as "Barbarossa," colored copper plate by Christian Siedentopf (1847)
p97	Henry VI: from *History of the German Emperors and Their Contemporaries* by Elizabeth Peake, p110; original held and digitized by the British Library, London
p99	Statue of Frederick II, Holy Roman Emperor, Royal Palace (Naples)
p100	Pages from *The Book of Falconry* by Frederick II, as they appear in *The Falconer* by Christopher Splendorio, copyright Waldorf Publications, 2010
p112	"Legend of St Francis, Sermon to the Birds," Saint Francis cycle in the Upper Church of San Francesco at Assisi, Italy) often attributed to Giotto but in dispute)
p113	"Vision de Jeanne d'Arc," in Domrémy in 1422, postcard, Épinal Municipal Library, France
p114	Section of frieze depicting the "The Life of Joan of Arc" (1890), Panthéon, Paris

Made in the USA
Middletown, DE
04 June 2025